Daily Youth Devotional

Daily Youth Devotional

Helping Teens Grow
Closer To God
One Day At A Time

Joel Wesseldyke

Foreword by Reverend Thomas C. Marsden

Daily Youth Devotions

Copyright © 2004 by Joel Wesseldyke, Yoot Press

All Scripture quotations, unless otherwise noted, are taken from the *Holy Bible: New International Version* ®. Copyright © 1973, 1978, 1984 by International Bible Society. Used by permission of Zondervan. All rights reserved.

The material in this book may be photocopied for local use in churches, youth groups, and other Christian-education activities. Special permission is not necessary. However, the contents of this book may not be reproduced in any other form without written permission from the publisher. All rights reserved.

Cover Design by: Kim Howell, Creative Samples, llc.
                    e-mail: Kim@CreativeSamples.com

Dedicated to the most loving parents in the world.

Mom,
Growing up, it was amazing to see
you live your life with a tremendous
sense of faith and Christian values.
Now that I'm "grown-up", I see
those things for what they are:
A blessing to me and everyone around you.

Dad,
You shared so much wisdom with me.
So many things that I would have had
to learn the hard way, but instead learned
from your solid example the difference between
right and wrong, even if I wasn't always able
To follow in your footsteps.

Thanks to you both, for letting me live and learn.
For teaching me what I thought I'd never need.
For giving me a solid Christian foundation.

Foreword

Finally, a daily devotional that speaks directly and plainly to the world of teenagers. Honest, personal, witty, and profound, each message holds the attention of the reader, challenging them to think about the things that really matter in their life, and to live out God's purpose, one day at a time.

Joel Wesseldyke is not afraid to deal with the day-to-day issues and questions of today's youth. This is a devotional, written specifically for teens, about life, relationships, struggles, pain, good times, and bad times, and how the message of the Scriptures holds hope and truths for today.

Joel has been blessed with the gift of being able to relate ancient, biblical truths to young people in a fresh, creative and thoughtful manner. The individual messages are pure Joel, flowing from his life, faith, and passion for leading young people to a deeper understanding of God's love and how His love through Jesus Christ manifests itself in daily life. His style is not preachy, but conversational and relational, connecting with his reader at a deeply personal level.

The contents of this book began as an experiment to reach the youth of Joel's church by sending out daily devotional thoughts, via the Internet, to those who registered their e-mail addresses. It quickly grew to a ministry of outreach, touching the lives of literally tens of thousands of young people throughout the United States. Daily, each person on his e-mail list receives a personalized electronic message of faith and hope, similar to those found in this devotional.

As Joel's pastor, I receive his daily e-mail messages and read them with great interest, as do many of my congregants. His insight into the day's passage is inspirational, and often crosses generational lines, touching our common humanity with practical spirituality.

The "Daily Youth Devotional" is an exceptional read and meditative tool and discussion starter. It is recommended, not just for teens, but pastors, youth directors, Christian Educators, and others working with youth in helping them to strengthen their faith and daily walk.

Rev. Thomas C. Marsden, Pastor
Old Paramus Reformed Church
Ridgewood, New Jersey

Day 1

> The man said, "The woman you put here with me -- she gave me some fruit from the tree, and I ate it." Then the Lord God said to the woman, "What is this you have done?" The woman said, "The serpent deceived me, and I ate."
>
> Genesis 3:12-13

Jump Off A Roof

How many times have you gotten in trouble for doing something you weren't supposed to do? If you're like me, you get in trouble more often than you'd like to admit.

Most of the time, when I get in trouble, I try to shift the blame. For example... Sometimes I make comments that are funny, but not very nice and I get in trouble for that. If I'm sitting next to someone, I might say, "He said it first" or "He said something and I had to respond"...

Most of the time, I still get in trouble, but I'm afraid of the punishment I'll get so I try to make it seem like it wasn't my fault. For your information, it never works, and I always get in trouble anyway...

So... If someone jumped off a roof, would you do it too?

When your parents are asking you this, what they're really asking you to do is take responsibility for your actions. To take your punishment for whatever you did and learn that every time you make that mistake there is a punishment that comes along with it...

This whole "Someone else made me do it" argument has been happening since the beginning of time! Adam and Eve tried to do it (and they didn't have any luck with it either... They still got punished) and people have been trying to shift blame ever since.

Making bad decisions is part of life. When we do it, we shift the blame because we're afraid. Always think carefully about your decisions and actions... Think about what you'll say if someone tells you it's OK to do something wrong... Even if it seems exciting. Remember that when your punishment comes around, you'll have to take responsibility for your actions.

Day 2

{ A simple man believes anything, but a prudent man gives thought to his steps. Proverbs 14:15 }

Even The Greatest

Even the greatest of whales is helpless in the desert. -- Confucius

Maybe you know someone who you consider wise. I know lots of wise people. My mom is very wise and before he passed away my dad was a very wise man. I've also had teachers, pastors and friends who were wise.

Wisdom comes with experience, which comes from living. One of my favorite phrases from my mom is: I've never seen a U-Haul behind a hearse. What she means is enjoy your money and possessions while you're alive because you can't take them with you when you die.

There's a lot of warmth in the sun

Sometimes my mom comes up with the obvious... But these things are truly wise thoughts. Through the years, she has learned a lot of valuable lessons. Not only does she pass on her wisdom to others, she applies everything she's learned throughout her lifetime to make good choices.

I think what this verse from Proverbs is telling us is without life experience and careful thought, we're likely to believe everything we hear and make poor decisions without thinking. But by paying attention to the lessons we learn throughout our lives we'll be able avoid some mistakes.

The great thing about wisdom is you can get more of it a couple ways... Living life and listening to other people and learning from them. I want to challenge you to do two things every day. Gain wisdom by living life with your eyes open (pay attention)... And listen to and learn from people who have more life experience than you.

Day 3

 For if you remain silent at this time, relief and deliverance for the Jews will arise from another place, but you and your father's family will perish. And who knows but that you have come to royal position for such a time as this? Esther 4:14

When Life Gives You Lemons

Maybe you've heard the phrase "When life gives you lemons make lemonade"... In other words, sometimes things happen in life that just stink... There's no other way to describe it... But when that's the case, make the best of the situation.

I was working for a company. I showed up every day, worked hard for the company. So did everyone else who worked there. But it wasn't enough. The company borrowed and spent a lot of money to get started, and no matter how hard everyone worked, couldn't pay back the money fast enough... And the company went out of business.

Maybe you've been in a similar situation. Maybe you've had a broken bone or been sick and were forced to stay inside. Maybe your family moved and you had to leave all your friends behind. Maybe a grandparent died. Whatever the case is, we've all had situations where life didn't seem so great.

Sometimes you just have to make the best of a bad situation

Sometimes life stinks. But good things can happen. In the examples above, I was out of a job... But got the opportunity to do what I've always dreamed of... Work with kids. So you broke a bone and had to stay in... Maybe you had a chance to read something you never would have. Your family moved... But you met a new best friend. Your grandparent passed away... But you were given something special to always remember them by.

Esther 4:14 is a little hard to figure out because there's background to the story. I'll give you the short version. One of the king's men wanted to kill all the Jews. Instead of running away, the Jews stayed where they were and really bad things happened to them... But God took care of them in the end. The king took back the order.

So for thousands of years, God has been helping people get through bad times and giving them good things in the end. So, when life gives you lemons... Make lemonade!

Day 4

 For such men are false apostles, deceitful workmen, masquerading as apostles of Christ. 2 Corinthians 11:13

Wolf In Sheep's Clothing

When I was in High School, I heard kids at school talking every Friday afternoon about the things they were going to be doing over the weekend. Parties, drinking, smoking, drugs, staying out really late and getting in trouble... All things I wasn't interested in.

Every Sunday in church and at Sunday school I heard all the adults praising these kids for being such great kids... "Why can't you be more like ... and stand up and profess your faith? Go through confirmation class, take the next step and be an active Christian in the church."

Every Monday morning I heard all the kids at school bragging about what they did and got away with over the weekend... Talking about how drunk they got, how they got one of the girls to have sex... That they were still hung over in church on Sunday morning, had been sick from all the drinking...

It's not about them... It's about you.

When I was about 16 I stopped going to church. Stopped being involved in the youth group, stopped talking to the adults in church, stopped talking to a lot of the kids at church and school... I had my circle of friends and that was it.

Why would I want to be a part of something where people were praised for being good Christians on Sunday and were the complete opposite of that on Monday? These kids were up in front of church telling everyone about how they were saved, how Jesus had made this huge difference in their lives. But not living like it.

I want to tell you a few things... Quitting church, Sunday school and youth group was not the answer. Christianity is personal... It's a relationship between you and God. Secondly, I want to challenge you to live a Christian life... Do the right thing on Sunday... Then again Monday through Saturday! Take a stand against these 'part time Christians' and show the world how a full time Christian lives.

Day 5

> Be careful to follow every command I am giving you today, so that you may live and increase and may enter and possess the land that the Lord promised on oath to your forefathers.
> Deuteronomy 8:1

While You Live Under My Roof

Curfews. No drinking. No smoking. Get a part time job. No fighting with your siblings. No talking back to your parents. Do your homework right away after school. Take out the trash. Do the dishes.

Maybe you have to obey some rules like this. When I was living with my parents, there were rules... I never broke them because I was a perfect child... But, even so... There were rules. I didn't always agree with them. I didn't always follow them. But there were rules, and they were enforced.

I can remember clearly my dad saying, "If you're going to live in my house, you're going to follow my rules. Period." There was no room for discussion... That was just the way it was. I quickly found out that the saying "Rules are meant to be broken" was not really such a good attitude to have.

Broken rules... Broken windows.

Even though it was hard to accept back then, my parents made these rules because they loved me and didn't want me to get hurt (or break windows with baseballs)... When I broke rules, there was a penalty involved... Maybe I had to pay for the broken window, or do some housework...

God has rules for us too... The Ten Commandments. He gave us these rules because he loves us. When we follow the rules, God blesses us. When we don't, He must punish us. None of us can keep the rules perfectly though... We all make mistakes. And that is why Jesus came to die on the cross. To take our punishment for sin.

Even though it's hard, remember that just like the rules our parents set up, the Ten Commandments are good for us. Try to follow both... And no matter what your parents tell you, 'thou shall not break windows with baseballs' is not the 11th commandment.

Day 6

> Nobody should seek his own good, but the good of others.
> 1 Corinthians 10:24

The Cool Crowd

"There's this cool party goin on at Cathi's house!" Sue said to Karen, a popular cheerleader... "All the cool people are gonna be there and since you're my one of my best friends we should go together!"

Karen wasn't Sue's best friend, or even close, but she figured that Karen was her ticket in to the party and a way for her to hang with and be part of the cool crowd... It could be her ticket out of the 'loser group' and help her become Miss Popularity!

Pretty selfish of Sue... Don't you think? This is just one example of selfish behavior, but there are lots... We're all selfish by nature. Television, music, and all other forms of media are pushing us to this with themes like "Take care of #1" and "What's in it for me?" in all the shows and commercials.

What's the benefit for them?

Often we do things for the wrong reasons... Whether we admit it or not, a lot of things we do could be considered selfish... Sometimes I do things for a specific reason, but it doesn't hurt that there is another benefit somewhere for me.

Corinthians tells us that it's important to do things thinking of other people, not of the benefit to us... A pretty tough task, I'd say... If we take out the trash for our parents, we should do it to help them out, not because maybe they'll let us stay out later on Friday night.

Be aware of your motives. Do something for someone today (and every day!) because you want to help them out, or are thinking of them... Not because of what it will do for you later on...

Day 7

> "Before I formed you in the womb I knew you, before you were born I set you apart; I appointed you as a prophet to the nations." "Ah Sovereign Lord," I said, "I do not know hot to speak; I am only a child." But the Lord said to me, "Do not say, 'I am only a child.' You must go to everyone I send you to and say whatever I command you. Do not be afraid of them, for I am with you and will rescue you," declares the Lord. Jeremiah 1:4-8

Whisper Or Scream

In some class I took, the teacher was telling us how to give a speech so that people really listen to what you're saying. He said that if a speaker uses a soft tone, people will really try to listen more.

I don't know about you, but when I'm watching TV and commercials come on, I'm more interested in a message from a quiet commercial than one with 'Fast Freddie' selling "ELECTRONICS AT BLOWOUT PRICES!!!" with sirens blaring and bright flashing colors.

When I think back to my favorite teachers, they had gentle voices... They were caring people who spoke to the class with such soothing voices... I also remember the teachers I didn't like... They yelled at us a lot... Maybe because we talked too much or because we had messy handwriting... Of course those are just examples... I didn't get yelled at for any of those things.

Are you hearing God's message?

There are really two messages in today's verse... One of them is we need to trust God and know that he will help you do His work. The second is God has a plan for your life.

God had a plan for Jeremiah before he was even born! It's amazing, isn't it? He has a plan for us! Think about it... God is whispering to us all our lives. He's putting us in situations where we have the opportunity to develop gifts and talents... He's not screaming at us because we don't listen to that.

Know that you are special to God and that He has a plan for your life. Pray today that God will begin to show you His plan for your life.

Day 8

> Then David said to Nathan, "I have sinned against the Lord." Nathan replied, "The Lord has taken away your sin. You are not going to die. 2 Samuel 12:13

Six Second Rule

I have a dog. A dog who doesn't always listen. If you have a dog or know someone who does you understand that even the best dogs don't always listen. It seems like Maggie, my dog, is an angel when I'm home, but is always getting in trouble when I'm not home.

Sometimes when I return from somewhere I find pillows torn apart and stuffing all over the floor... I come home to find clothes all over the place... Or find her playing with trash from the garbage can... Sometimes I even find an 'accident' if she was left home alone too long. She gets bored, I guess, or maybe is trying to tell me how mad she is that I left her alone...

Unfortunately, since I rarely catch the dog doing something bad, I can't really get mad at her and forgiveness soon follows. There are a million dog experts who say that a dog only understands why it's being punished if you catch it within 6 seconds of the bad behavior... Since that almost never happens, she's back on my good side quickly.

You are forgiven

God has rules for us... The Ten Commandments, remember? They are Gods laws for how we're supposed to live. Of course, sometimes we're going to break God's rules... That's just the way it is... We're human and imperfect.

Sure, the 'Six Second Rule' isn't quite the same with God, and us but the fact is, we can get back on God's 'good side' by asking for His forgiveness... There are penalties for breaking the rules, but once we truly ask for it, we're forgiven...

Thank God today for His love and mercy. Tell Him about the mistakes you made... Tell Him you are truly sorry for your mistakes and ask for forgiveness. God is a loving and forgiving God who never stays mad at us for long... He follows the 'Six Second Rule" too!

Day 9

> Once when Jacob was cooking some stew, Esau came in from the open country, famished. He said to Jacob, "Quick, let me have some of that red stew! I'm famished!" Jacob replied, "First sell me your birthright." "Look, I'm about to die," Esau said. "What good is the birthright to me?" Genesis 25:29-32

The Value Of A Sandwich

I love sandwiches. Chicken, turkey, burgers, cheese steaks... All kinds of sandwiches... But my favorite type of sandwich is a Reuben. Corn beef, sauerkraut, cheese... Yummy! It's high in taste... I love em! But it's also high in cholesterol, carbs, fat, oil and lets not forget... Calories.

I'm always on a diet. Always struggling to lose weight. It's always a battle (a losing one!), but I decided I was going to really work hard at my diet and take the pounds off for good. There are a lot of reasons why I should take off the pounds... I'd be healthier, more energetic, look better, and feel better... Like I said... Lots of reasons.

But I always start off watching what I eat carefully. Only one serving, no sugar, none of the other bad stuff... But Eventually, I give up and cheat... Gotta have one of those brownies! The reason I can't stick with a diet is because I lose sight of the end result. I need immediate results. I want to stop eating bad food today and wake up tomorrow 50 pounds lighter. Of course that doesn't work.

What's your sandwich?

Maybe you know the story of Jacob and Esau. I thought I did, too. Then I went back and really thought about it... Esau is just like me. He wanted immediate results and didn't really care about the long-term effects. He gave up something very important for a bowl of soup because he was hungry!

Maybe you don't struggle with food like I do, but I bet there are times when you forget about the long term and make a decision or do something that brings you immediate results. We all do!

Get in the habit of thinking about the long-term effects right now. If something is really worth eating (or doing) it will fall in to your long-term plan. Don't take short cuts and give up things that may be important down the road...

Day 10

> In the thirty-ninth year of his reign, Asa was afflicted with a disease in his feet. Though his disease was severe, even in his illness he did not seek help from the Lord, but only from physicians. 2 Chronicles 16:12

I Have An Owie!

The screech was deafening... Enough to make the dog wake up and see what all the noise was about (but not enough for her to get up and help, apparently). The screech was followed by a whirlwind run through the living room, into the bathroom where the first-aid kit is located.

I was cooking dinner... In a hurry, as always, I sliced the top of a package open... Along with my finger... A pretty deep cut, I'd say. I ran my finger under water before applying a towel and direct pressure to stop the bleeding before putting on a bandage...

Fortunately, my cut didn't send me to the emergency room... I've been to the emergency room... It isn't a good time. If you've been to the hospital, you know what I'm talking about... Long lines, lots of people who are hurt and sick, upset families...

Who'll kiss your boo-boo?

If you read the whole chapter in 3 Chronicles, I think you'll see that Asa's illness is a form of punishment. And that he couldn't be healed by doctors until he apologized for his sins. He didn't cut his finger while carelessly opening a package, but he wasn't very smart either.

Anyway, I like to look at the abilities of doctors as a blessing from God. God works through doctors to fix our aches and pains (or our cut fingers!) so without God, the people in the hospitals wouldn't be able to fix you at all.

Don't ever forget who the greatest 'doctor' is... God is able to heal cut fingers, broken bones, all forms of diseases and everything else that could be wrong with us... Take time today (and every day!) to remember friends, family, church members and everyone else who need God's healing power.

Day 11

 Do not gloat when your enemy falls; when he stumbles, do not let your heart rejoice, or the Lord will see and disapprove and turn his wrath away from him.
Proverbs 24:17-18

Did You Know?

I'm colorblind? I'm clumsy? I'm a fashion nightmare? Sometimes I'm not that smart? Most of the time I don't know where I'm supposed to be? My hair isn't ever combed? Most of the time I look like I just rolled out of bed? I'm not very good at sports?

It's true... All of it... A lot of times my clothes don't match, I'm wearing two different colored socks, I knock stuff over (or drop stuff) everywhere I go... You get the point. None of this is new for me though; I've always been all of these things.

When I was a teenager, I got laughed at a lot. For all of these reasons, and lots of others. I can tell you one thing... The memories that are the clearest from back then are ones where I did something other people thought was stupid and laughed at me.

What memories are you creating?

Looking back now, I can say that I got laughed at a lot, but I laughed at and teased people who I thought weren't as good as me... There weren't that many, admittedly, but I was just as guilty of creating bad memories for some people as anyone. If people were laughing WITH me at someone else, they weren't laughing AT me.

I tell you this because most of us are guilty of doing this, no matter how popular we are... Just think about how you feel when people laugh at you for tripping, or wearing a shirt that was out of style last year, or whatever else you might get laughed at for...

How about when you laughed at someone else? What did they do to deserve that? How do you think they felt being laughed at? Just remember that God sees our actions and doesn't like it when we tease someone else... What will you do the next time someone making a mistake?

Day 12

> When a man makes a vow to the Lord or takes an oath to obligate himself by a pledge, he must not break his word but must do everything he said. Numbers 30:2

Make The Call

There is nothing more frustrating to me than when someone promises to do something for me then doesn't follow through with their promise.

I remember a time when I was shopping in a music store. I wanted four inexpensive cymbals... Three of them they had in the store, the fourth they didn't carry, but could special order for me. The sales person promised he would call the maker of the cymbal I want, find out how much it costs and call me so I could decide whether to order it or not.

Well, I'm still waiting for the phone call. I'm beginning to think the sales person isn't going to call the company or even call me. He promised me he would call the company and let me know about the cymbal I wanted... And he didn't. If he had no intention of doing it, why did he tell me he would? Why do people do that?!

When you make a promise... Follow through.

How often do you make promises and fail to follow through with them? I'm as guilty as anyone... I promise to be in class on time, get work done on time, keep a date, to call... All these promises are made with good intentions... I plan to do all of them... But I don't follow through with them. (Except when it's something important like cymbals!)

Maybe you do the same thing... Promise to study more, do dishes, take out garbage, or mow the lawn... How long do you think it takes for someone to think your promises don't mean anything? Is that the reputation you want to have with your parents, teachers, friends? With anyone??

Numbers 30 tells us the importance of keeping promises... What can you do to keep your promises? Maybe think carefully about whether you can keep the promise before making it? Or just go the extra step to keep the promises you make? Make the decision today to follow through with your promises.

Day 13

 Then Jesus said to Simon, "Don't be afraid; from now on you will catch men." So they pulled their boats up on shore, left everything and followed him. Luke 5:10b-11

Catching Any Fish?

Did you happen to see the Super Bowl in 2004? Maybe you did... Maybe you didn't. But, I'm sure you heard about it... Right? Well, maybe you didn't hear about the game, but I bet you heard about things that happened at half time of the game...

I can't even believe how fast the news of what happened spread. Whether or not you think what happened was the most terrible thing ever or that it wasn't that big of a deal, one thing is for sure... Everyone was talking about it... Even a long time after it happened, many people still are!

OK... This isn't a current event... This happened a long time ago... But thinking about what happened, and how everyone was talking about it made me wonder about something... Why does some news travel really fast, and some news travel so much slower?

What's REALLY News

Today's message from Luke has a lot of great things to say... Someday I'll get into it more, but I chose this section because like Simon and the rest of the disciples, we're supposed to tell people about Jesus. Now that's a good news story!

I know that I've written before about telling people what we know... But sometimes I think it doesn't sink in. Sometimes I think even though we know what we're supposed to do, we don't. There are so many ways to spread this great news... Are you doing your part?

Think about how fast the news of what happened at the Super Bowl spread ... Now think about how easy it is for us to spread good news. Even something as simple as inviting your friends to church or youth group could make a difference in their lives. Ask God today how you can spread his word to all your friends and family... I know you'll do your part to spread the good news.

Day 14

> I also want women to dress modestly, with decency and propriety, not with braided hair or gold or pearls or expensive clothes. 1 Timothy 2:9

Has Fashion Gone Too Far?

I love the mall. I hate shopping for clothes and other stuff (bring on the video games!) but I love watching people. I could sit on the benches for hours just watching people walk by. People of all ages, shapes and sizes are there by themselves, with family, with friends... All walking around from store to store.

Sometimes I look around and see how much stuff has changed from when I was in junior high and high school. Young men and women laughing and talking with their friends, flirting with the opposite sex, all dressed up and looking so... Adult. Fashion in particular has really changed over the years.

Young women wear really tight tops with really low necklines... Jeans that were so tight I can't even imagine how they got into them, riding low on the hips... The guys are just as bad with pants hanging way down, shirts open half way down their chest...

So... What's Appropriate?

So today, I want you to think about modesty. The verse for today is pretty strict, I'd say... And really has no place in today's world... I mean... Come on... No braided hair? That seems a little strict, doesn't it? There's nothing wrong with being fashionable, stylish and looking good...

So, like everything, we have to take these words and try to apply them to modern times... Paul wrote these words, and in his day, these were reasonable things... Today they really aren't. But, there has to be some kind of middle ground. Some amount of modesty.

Think about what's in your closet. Find the middle ground between "no braided hair" and displaying everything for the world to see. Sometimes there's more to looking good than following the fashion trends... A little thing called modesty goes a long way.

Day 15

> So the Pharisees and teachers of the law asked Jesus, "Why don't your disciples live according to the tradition of the elders instead of eating their food with 'unclean' hands?"
> Mark 7:5

Routines

My life is ruled by routine. Every morning, I roll out of bed, go to the restroom, make a pot of coffee, turn on the Today Show, check and write e-mail, take a shower, brush my teeth and go about my day.

You probably have routines that you follow too. Without routines and schedules, our days would be crazy and nothing would ever get done! I'd be perfectly content to sit and play video games all day and have no set routine (maybe that's a routine too!) but I wouldn't get any work done.

If I'm being honest, maybe my routines include religion. Praying first thing in the morning, before eating and before going to bed. Studying the Bible in the evenings... These are all things that I've done for years... But why? I guess because I've always done it that way. It's a routine.

Is Christianity part of a routine?

I hope you take the time to read Mark 7 today. I picked one verse from it, but the story continues with Jesus calling the Pharisees hypocrites who worship out of routine, not out of love for God. Jesus says they worship in vain because they follow rules taught by men.

So when the disciples eat with 'unclean hands' they're not following the traditions and routines, but it doesn't matter because their hearts are in the right place for worship.

Take a look at your routines and schedules. It's good to have them, but make sure they don't get in the way of your time with God. I hope that even though you may have routines, where your relationship with God is concerned, your heart is in the right place.

Day 16

> He said to another man, "Follow me." But the man replied, "Lord, first let me go and bury my father." Luke 9:59

National Procrastination Week

Last week was 'National Procrastination week'. I meant to tell you last week, but I just didn't get around to it. It's a regular holiday in my house... Everyday is 'National Procrastination Day'. Because I put off getting stuff done. Most of the time there is nothing so important that it absolutely must get done today... Even though there are some times when something's really do need to get done... Today.

Procrastination means to delay action. I don't know about you, but I'm one of those people who waits until the last minute to get something done. When I have a big paper due for one of my classes, I almost never work on it until the morning it's due... Most of the time I don't even THINK about it until the night before!

I can think of a lot of examples of how I put things off... Can you? Maybe you wait until the last minute to get homework done, maybe you put off taking out the trash, maybe you make excuses to wait a little longer before going to bed or taking out the dog...

No more 'National Procrastination week'

There are lots of examples of procrastination in the Bible. In today's verse, men were making excuses to get out of following Jesus. One said he would follow, but not until after he buried his father. Another, later in the chapter said, he wanted to go and say goodbye to his family.

Jesus said, "No one who puts his hand to the plow and looks back is fit for service in the kingdom of God." What he's saying, I think, is that if you're going to be a Christian and do the work of the Lord, there aren't any reasons to start tomorrow or even later today. Start now!

I'll always wait until the last minute to do my work, and everyone else will put off doing the things they don't like. We just can't put off the important things. As Christians, we have work to do... Work that can't wait until later.

Day 17

 We are therefore Christ's ambassadors, as though God were making his appeal through us. We implore you on Christ's behalf: Be reconciled to God. 2 Corinthians 5:20

Flat Tire

Have you ever been riding in a car that suddenly had a flat tire? If you have, you'll never forget the feeling of having a car lunge to the side and the clatter that it makes while the driver, whether it's you or someone else, is trying to keep the car under control. Obviously you can't drive very well with a flat tire.

A car with a flat tire can't do what it was intended to do... Get you from place to place. The car just doesn't feel right... Doesn't drive right with a flat. But moving you quickly to where you want to go is it's only purpose. So what happens? The tire gets changed, and you're back on the road.

I don't know about you, but sometimes I feel like I have a flat tire. I feel like I'm unable to do what God put me on this earth to do. Sometimes I feel out of control... Like I'm not doing my job as well as I could... And I just want to scream, "Where have I gone wrong?!"

We're ambassadors

An ambassador is someone who speaks on behalf of another higher-ranking person. We're God's ambassadors. It's our job to speak to other people on Gods behalf. God wants to be a part of everyone's life. He wants to talk to all of them, but sometimes it takes someone else, like us, to get people to listen!

Now, for me, this has a special meaning because it's my full time job to teach people about God. And even when I feel like I have a flat tire, I have to remember that I'm speaking for God right here on earth!

But you know, it applies to you as well. No matter what your job is, whether it's school, or washing cars, or sweeping floors... Anything at all... You're sometimes going to feel like you have a flat tire. But remember that no matter what you're doing, you have a more important job, and God will give you the strength to fix your flat tire and get you back on the road.

Day 18

> A happy heart makes the face cheerful, but heartache crushes the spirit. Proverbs 15:13

Attitude Adjustment

In about two week, I somehow managed to give two of my professors the impression that I didn't like them or the classes they teach. I forced them to use their authority in the classroom and seem like they were trying to make life difficult for me.

I'd like to think that I'm not usually like that. I try to get along with everyone, make the best of a situation and work hard in class. So the fact that two teachers were put in an uncomfortable situation because of either something I said, or my body language makes me feel bad.

I sat in those classes and grumbled about how petty the teachers were being. How silly it was to take that tone with me, an older student... "I'm not an 18 year old freshman who needs to have his hand held... What's wrong with these people?" I thought...

Attitude Adjustment Necessary

I was reading this verse in Proverbs today. And it came to me... It wasn't the teachers who had the problem it was me! Something I did or said was taken a certain way and the teacher had to react to that. Once in a while things like this happen... But two in a couple weeks? That's very unusual for me.

Maybe you've had similar situations. Maybe you're feeling stressed out... Mad at your friends... Frustrated with your parents. Don't want to be in a certain class... And one of those people says something to you about the way you're handling that situation. Maybe you get angry, yell at them or show your frustration in some other way.

I'm here to tell you that sometimes we all need attitude adjustments. If you're in a frustrating situation, decide to change your attitude and make the best of it... A change in your attitude may not change the situation, but can definitely make you feel better.

Day 19

 [People] who say, "Keep away; don't come near me, for I am too sacred for you!" are smoke in my nostrils, a fire that keeps burning all day. Isaiah 65:5

I'm Better Than You

Lately there have been an awful lot of people who think they're better than others. White people who think they're better than Asian people, Hispanic people who think they're better than another culture. Athletes who think they're better than good students. Smart people who think they're better than the geeks...

This isn't something new. For years there have been different classes of people, different levels of popularity, a feeling of superiority among groups of people... Sometimes it even goes the other way... A certain group feels like they're less popular or more likely to be picked on than another.

Lately, I've been noticing that these attitudes are popping up more often. Sure, even when I was in high school the athletes and cheerleaders were more popular than the drama kids or the smart kids, but lately it seems like as much as that's a problem, there are groups of people who feel like they're being picked on...

Who's better?

No matter what side of the 'argument' you're on, whether it's "I'm better than those people" or "Those people are better than I am", I think it's important to remember that we're all created in God's image. We're all equal in God's eyes. Made just the way God wants us.

In today's verse, people who have the 'I'm better than you' attitude will be punished. Later on in the chapter, these people are told they'll lose battles, be hungry, thirsty and be put to shame.

Maybe sometimes you fall into the trap of thinking you're better than another group, or you have a 'chip on your shoulder' and think other people are better than you... My challenge for you today is to remember that we're all equal and should strive to get along with everyone no matter what group we belong to because we're all created just the way God wanted us.

Day 20

> "Then Naomi took the child, laid him in her lap and cared for him." Ruth 4:16

Grandma's

Grandmas are pretty amazing people. Whether you call them Nanna, Gram, Gramma... Whatever, they're amazing. I happen to know two amazing grandmothers. My mom, who has what seems like 100 grandchildren who adore her, and my dearest friend, Mrs. Oatmeal...

You might be wondering what grandma's have to do with anything, so I'll tell ya... One day I walked in to church and a baby was amusing all the people in the office. (Why is it that no work gets done in an office when there's a baby around?) Turns out, it was Jack, Mrs. Oatmeal's grandson. He was pretty content... Until he ended up in my arms.

Now, I've been around babies my whole life... I love em! And I'm usually pretty good at keeping them from crying, but Jack just wasn't having any fun. He cried. Then stopped for a sec (to breath, apparently) then wailed again. He was just not happy, and no matter what I did, Jack just kept on crying.

Sometimes it takes a Nanna to fix it

Well, wouldn't you know, Mrs. Oatmeal took Jack and walked away and he stopped crying immediately. She had the magic touch! She took cute little Jack and made it all better. When I went to see what happened, I found out she had just what Jack wanted... A bottle.

I think feeding and caring for babies is part of something called "nurturing"... There are lots of places in the Bible where people are nurtured. This instance, in Ruth, Naomi is caring for her son, Obed.

Sometimes we just need to be "nurtured". It can come from parents, grandparents, youth leaders, teachers... Anyone. It's just that extra little love that comes when we need it. Grandmas were put here by God to give us that extra shot of love just when we need it.

Day 21

{ Can a man walk on hot coals without his feet being scorched? Proverbs 6:28 }

Quiz

Quiz: What do grocery stores, the Internet, television, advertisements, movies, music and magazines all have in common?

These things seem pretty random, right? But they all have something in common. They all contain things that tempt us. You can't walk down the magazine aisle in the store without seeing half naked men and women on the covers. You can't turn on television without seeing scantily clad people... The Internet? Forget it...

Everywhere we go, we're shown very sexual images. In music, we hear about sexual topics and see them on the CD covers... How are we supposed to avoid thinking about sex when everywhere we turn there are things that tempt us to think about it?

Be strong!

Once I visited a youth group at another church. They were presenting a series of messages called "True Love Waits". They were talking about how these sexual images are everywhere... I never really thought about it, but it's true! Now... Is it wrong for us to look at these images? They don't have to be in explicit magazines or movies to have sexual content. Even the music, magazines, PG movies, and other "mainstream" things have stuff that could tempt us. Including network TV!

Today's verse talks about the problem with temptation. If you give in to the temptation of looking at these images, how long will it take before you give in to the actual act? At this True Love Waits seminar, the speaker said something that makes sense: just look away!

If we stop supporting those types of shows, music, movies, and magazines there won't be a reason to make them... Because nobody would be buying them! I want to challenge you to turn your eyes away from the magazine covers, the scenes in movies, the advertisements on the Internet. Just turn away! Don't even put yourself in a position to be tempted!

Day 22

> My heart is steadfast, O God, my heart is steadfast; I will sing and make music. Psalm 57:7

Your Own Beat

You may know that I play the drums. I'm fanatical about it. I love playing along with my favorite songs or just making up my own rhythms. As a drummer, one of the hardest things to do is play off the main beat of the song... But it sounds amazing if it's done right.

Most music you hear on the radio doesn't use these kinds of rhythms because they don't sound normal. They don't fit into most popular music today... Not to mention it's hard to go against what's normal. It's not the kind of thing that you hear once and instantly love and remember... So that kind of music never gets on the radio!

If you ever hear music like this, you'd know it though... You're forced to listen because it's not quite normal... It sounds unusual and may even sound wrong. But the more you listen, the more you get caught up in this off beat drumming... It's unique!

Be your own drummer

Maybe drums are a metaphor for our lives as Christians. It's much easier to go with the crowd. To be one of the gang... To be "normal" in the eyes of our friends. It's very hard and not cool to be on the outside of these groups. To look and sound different is not what we strive to do with our friends.

It's hard to live on the off beat when everyone else is living a certain way... Psalm 57:7 talks about praising God all the time... In all our actions, we're to praise God for his goodness and mercy. Whether we're speaking, singing, walking, hanging with friends... No matter what, we're supposed to live differently than non-Christians... Because when we do, people will notice...

I know it's hard... Believe me... But strive to live on the off beat... Praise God in everything you do. Anyone can play on the beat... It takes someone special to play off the beat.

Day 23

 For whoever does the will of my Father in heaven is my brother and sister and mother." Matthew 12:50

Amazing Kid Day

There's a day in the spring, March 18, that is National Amazing Kid Day. Really... I didn't make it up. It's not a government holiday, you don't get a day off from school, no special lunches, no special privileges... But it is a holiday that I'm proud to celebrate, and I hope you will too.

I tell you this, along with today's verse from Matthew, because... Frankly... Every day should be National Amazing Kid Day... And in celebrating this holiday and every day together as Christians, we're brothers and sisters... Sorta...

Now, being a youth worker, I see all the great things young people do every day... I see kids doing service projects, helping out with chores around the house, telling people... Either by words or actions, they're Christians... There are tons of great things young people do every day...

Do You Know An Amazing Kid?

I bet you do. No matter how old you are, I'm sure you know an amazing kid... Maybe someone who does the things I mentioned... Maybe they do other things... Maybe they just make it a habit of being supportive and building up people around them.

Whatever those amazing kids do, they are our brothers and sisters in Christ... And today... Well, every day, really... We should take time to let those kids know that they're amazing!

Go out of your way today to tell someone you know that they're amazing... Take good care of your brothers and sisters and build them up... Let them know that whatever they're doing that makes them amazing is being noticed...

Day 24

{ But now trouble comes to you, and you are discouraged; it strikes you and you are dismayed. Job 4:5 }

Look In A Mirror

Sometimes sadness sneaks up on us without warning. Maybe something happened to us, or to someone we know... Maybe we lost a loved one or got news that someone we love has an illness. Maybe it's nothing that serious... Maybe the sports team we love has a terrible season.

Sometimes we get sad and look to people like parents, teachers, pastors maybe even friends or coaches for support. Someone to help us feel better. For me, it's my mom. I can always count on her to make me feel better...

What happens when that person is having a bad day? We need them to help us feel better... The person you look to for strength is having a bad day and now you start to wonder... "Is that person just telling me things to make me feel better?"

Hypocrite!

Do you know what the word hypocrite means? It's really just someone who tells you things but doesn't follow their own advice or believe in the things they say... So... When Alan Trammel, the coach of the Tigers, says, "This year is going to be different than the last 20 years..." He's probably being a hypocrite... OK... It's a coach's job to make everyone feel better and encourage his team, so that's not fair... But you get the idea.

Job was a prophet in the Old Testament. He went around telling everyone about God, even though the people were having so many problems. When he went through some tough times, he caved and started saying and doing things that went against what he was teaching everyone else. So he was being a hypocrite!

As Christians, we go out and try to encourage people, try to teach them about God and Jesus. Try to explain that even though sometimes bad things happen, it's for a reason... We all get sad sometimes. That's the way life goes... Just keep your faith strong... Because there are lots of people listening and watching you and you don't want them to think you're a hypocrite just because you're having a bad day...

Day 25

 Though one may be overpowered, two can defend themselves.
A cord of three strands is not quickly broken.
Ecclesiastes 4:12

1 Is The Loneliest Number

One really is the loneliest number... I remember when I was in school, I sometimes felt like I didn't have any friends who understood me or my values. I was more interested in computers than going out with friends... More interested in doing the right thing than doing drugs or drinking alcohol.

Because of that, I spent lots of hours alone. Pretty sad, really. I could have done things differently, been more popular, made more friends... But who needed friends that didn't feel the same way about things as me?

I'll tell you what started this whole thought for today's message. I was talking to a teenager from church... He was telling me how hard it is to stay strong and do the right thing when all his friends are doing things that he doesn't agree with... And he feels like he's alone.

The joy of the Internet

I started thinking that if I had this problem a long time ago, and this guy is having the same thing today... He must not be alone. Maybe you're feeling the same type of pressure... Maybe you feel like you're all alone and don't have any friends...

So I started looking in the Bible for some encouragement... I came up with today's verse... Two (or three or ten) is better than one. A group of people with the same ideas and lifestyles are really friends that you want to be around.

The great thing about the Internet is that it brings people from all over the world with similar ideas and lifestyles together... Like our OPRCYouth! family... There are a tremendous number of people who all share your love of Jesus... Why not reach out to them? What a perfect way to ease the loneliness when you feel like it's you against the world.

Day 26

> Death and destruction are never satisfied, and neither are the eyes of man. Proverbs 27:20

Nine Lives

Have you ever heard the expression "Cats have nine lives?" People say this because cats are so curious about things... They're always checking stuff out, and often it gets them in trouble... And often they get out of these situations, so they must have 9 lives!

I'm pretty curious about things... Always trying to figure out how things work, how to take them apart... And how to put them back together, which almost never works... I always end up with spare parts!

Curiosity can be a good thing. That's what inspires us to learn new things... After all, if I wasn't curious to know how televisions work, I wouldn't have taken the cover off the back to check it out!

Watch out for the shock

Of course, the flaw in being curious is that unlike cats, we don't always have the ability to get out of bad situations... So we have to use a little common sense... Something I sometimes lack, by the way...

Take for example, the television... Did you know that there's a part in there that holds thousands of volts of electricity even when it's not plugged in? I didn't... Until I bumped it with a piece of metal and blew up the TV... That could have been dangerous! (There goes another one of my 9 lives)...

Proverbs tells us that we'll always be curious... And it's a good thing! I don't want to encourage you to stop being curious about things because then you'll stop learning... But... I want you to exercise caution when you're trying to figure something out... There are a lot of people who need you alive and well!

Day 27

> Commit to your Lord whatever you do, and your plans will succeed. Proverbs 16:3

Going, Going, Gone!

I love Spring. But not for the reasons most people do. Sure, the weather gets warmer, grass is green, trees start getting leaves, here on the East Coast the snow melts... All those things are great but I love Spring because of one thing... Baseball season is starts... Each Spring (and for the next few months) my whole schedule revolves around baseball. When laundry gets done, when I take out the dog, when I get groceries, when I go out with friends... All scheduled around the Yankees schedule.

You could say I'm fanatical about it, and I guess you'd be right. I got cable just so I'd be able to watch all the games on television. When I'm in the car, I listen on the radio... I read the news articles about the players, search the website for information and watch the highlights on the news.

There aren't too many things I'm this crazy about... That I would completely adjust my schedule for... But baseball has a special place in my life. I'm committed to the Yankees.

Are you fanatical?

I'm sure that you have something you're this involved with... A sports team, music group, television show, video game, hobby... God...

There are a lot of places in the Bible where people are 100% committed to God... We should be as committed to God as we are to our favorite pass times... Hard to imagine, isn't it?

I want to encourage you to do the same thing I do... Schedule time with God every day. I know you're busy... We all are... But I know you can find 10 minutes in your day to pray or read the Bible... Think about how much scheduling you do to watch your favorite show... If you spent a small amount of energy finding time for God you'd be surprised how easy it is to find...

Day 28

> Do not let any unwholesome talk come out of your mouths, but only what is helpful for building others up according to their needs, that it may benefit those who listen.
> Ephesians 4:29

Cruelty To

People are sometimes cruel. Wow... There's a news flash, right? Here's another... Some people take great pleasure in making other people feel bad. Want one more? Some people swear and use bad language because they think it makes them cool.

I know what you're thinking... "Gee, Captain Obvious... That is ground breaking information. I never would have known that without you pointing it out." Well... Cut me a break here... I know you've heard this all before... Maybe you've experienced it first hand...

Everywhere I go, everything I see on television, and everything I hear on the radio... People are picking on each other. They're making really mean comments, just cutting each other down... And for no real reason. But this is what we see, and somehow it becomes acceptable... It even becomes expected!

Cruelty to people

You know, what really bothers me is that there are no penalties for "cruelty to people"... Well, not when the cruelty comes in the form of verbal abuse... When people are mean, it hurts so much more than anyone realizes. People's whole personalities are sometimes made up of how other people treat them. If they get picked on, it may cause low self-esteem...

Besides the fact that cruel words make people feel bad, and people who swear might be offending others, I think it really shows a lack of intelligence... I mean, if all a person can do is tear people apart with words or curse all the time, it shows a lack of ability to be smart enough to think of other ways to express themselves.

Think about all the things that you say to people every day... Do you treat people kindly? What kind of things do you think a Christian would never say? What are some things a Christian would say to other people? Ask God to give you the sensitivity to be kind to people.

Day 29

{ "In your anger do not sin": Do not let the sun go down while you are still angry. Ephesians 4:26 }

Up To Here

I sometimes frustrate people. Sometimes people frustrate me. Sometimes it goes beyond frustration and people are really mad at me. I wish I could say I didn't deserve that, but the truth is... Sometimes I do things that make people angry. How about you?

A phrase comes to mind... "I've had it up to here!"... Sometimes I've seen it on television, I've had teachers that have used this phrase, I've read it in books... What does it mean? The person saying this is saying they're getting frustrated (or mad) and just can't take any more.

How's this for a spin on anger... Maybe there's a positive side to it... Maybe anger comes from an extreme passion about something. I don't get angry very often, but when I do, it's because someone I love is doing something that I don't approve of... I'm passionate about someone not swearing around me... And when they do, I get angry.

Let it go!

You know, sometimes we all get angry... Maybe about important things, maybe about silly things. But we all get frustrated with other people or situations... It's just part of life.

I'd like to give you two pieces of advice about keeping your anger under control... Don't do something bad when you're angry... For example, if you're mad because you dropped some money, don't rob a bank... And the second thing is maybe the best advice anyone has ever given me: don't go to bed angry. If you're mad resolve it...

There are going to be times when you're so mad you can't think straight. There are going to be times when people are mad at you... Keep all these emotions under control and in perspective... Understand that most of the little frustrations of life are just that... Little.

Day 30

> Yet at the same time many even among the leaders believed in him. But because of the Pharisees they would not confess their faith for fear they would be put out of the synagogue; for they loved praise from men more than praise from God.
> John 12:42-43

Afraid Of You

Often the people with the loudest voices get heard; people who are persistent get things done; people who can put pressure on another person is likely to get what they want... Does this seem right to you?

Maybe you've seen evidence of this in the news. There are lots of examples, but a couple come immediately to mind. I'm not making judgment (saying one way or the other is right and wrong) just pointing something out for you. You can and should form your own opinions about everything.

There are huge groups of people arguing both sides in these two examples: same sex marriage and war. This is an election year in the United States, so the politicians are trying to get elected by claiming to agree with the largest group of voters, without offending the rest of the people who don't agree.

Strength in numbers!

In today's verse from John, the leaders are so terrified of the Pharisees that even though they believe in Jesus, they don't make it public because they're afraid of the consequences!

How is that any different than politicians today? What kind of person are you if privately you support the war effort, but publicly claim to be against it? It's all because of the power of people. Just like it was in the Bible... That doesn't make it right, but it is a fact. A large group of people holds power that individuals do not.

So... If, as a Christian, you think you can't make a difference... Look around you! There are lots of other Christians fighting battles every day, and the more people who speak up, the more likely their opinion will be heard... There's power in numbers! Join or support a group with the same opinions and goals as you do and watch for change!

Day 31

 "I establish my covenant with you: Never again will all life be cut off by the waters of a flood; never again will there be a flood to destroy the earth." Genesis 9:11

It's Rainin!

It's raining, raining on the streets of New York City... Rainin, rainin... Rain is fallin down from heaven... OK... A little random... But it's a line from a great song... And it fits quite often... It's rains a lot on the East Coast.

I love rain. Sometimes I think about how much it rains. Where does all the water go? It rains for days at a time and it seems like there's always an area that floods. But, over all I think rain is so soothing and relaxing.

Maybe it's the rhythm of the drops hitting things. I don't know, but it's so relaxing to hear rain hit the windows... What a blessing rain is! It helps make things beautiful. Washes away dirt (for those of us who don't believe in car washes), makes things grow... Without rain we'd be in serious trouble.

Another promise kept

I also love thunder and lightning. What an awesome display of power from God... I watch the news, hoping to see thundershowers on the radar for the upcoming days... And I love the surprise afternoon showers with the huge cracks of thunder and bolts of electricity slashing through the sky.

But just imagine what it must have been like with the flood described in Genesis. Can you imagine that much rain? Can you imagine being locked up in a boat for so long, hearing the rain? I love hearing rain and storms, but I know there'll be an end to it and at the end, everything will go right back to normal!

When it's raining I get up and thank God for the rain, and all the blessings that come along with it. And for keeping his promise: no more floods that destroy the world. Take time today to thank God for all the wonderful things in nature that he provides for us... And for keeping all his promises.

Day 32

> "Say to the daughter of Zion, 'See, your king comes to you, gentle and riding on a donkey, on a colt, the foal of a donkey.'" Matthew 21:5

Tulips Are Blooming

Every year in the Spring, Holland, Michigan hosts a huge festival... Tulip Time. Thousands and thousands of people come to see these tulips, bands marching in parades, Dutch dancers... All kinds of festivities... And lets not forget junk food!

Parades are pretty cool. Whether you're at Tulip Time, the Rose Bowl, Thanksgiving Day, or any of the other hundreds of parades, the thrill of being there is being around all the people... All the energy and excitement is catching!

There was one sermon in particular that caught my attention... Reverend Marsden, the pastor at Old Paramus Reformed Church, was preaching a fantastic sermon that really hit home for me, which is why I'm borrowing the thoughts from it... He was talking about parades.

Hero to zero... In a week?

Now, I'm not sure this was Rev. Marsden's point... But I walked away from that church service thinking... "Wow... The people were all excited about Jesus' entrance... and at the end of the week, they crucified him! How does that happen?"

I don't have all the answers... I study just like you do... But I think that maybe all the excitement over Jesus was part of the same thing that happens at big parades today. The excitement was catching... The people were all yelling and cheering... It was a party! They may not have even realized what they were really cheering for. They were part of a cheering crowd, and the natural thing to do is yell and cheer along with the crowd!

It's hard to know what really happened way back then... I don't claim to know, Rev. Marsden doesn't know for certain... But I know one thing for sure... I'm a cheerleader for Jesus every day of my life, through my words and actions... And I hope you are too... I hope you live a Christian life with the excitement that's normally found at parades.

Day 33

 He replied, "I have been very zealous for the Lord God Almighty. The Israelites have rejected your covenant, broken down your altars, and put your prophets to death with the sword. I am the only one left, and now they are trying to kill me too." 1 Kings 19:10

The Glass Is...

Sometimes life stinks. Maybe your teachers aren't being fair, maybe your parents aren't treating you as the young-adult you are, maybe things just aren't going your way... Whatever your specific situation, sometimes life just stinks... Or does it?

Even though it annoys people, I try to see the positive side of everything. Maybe I can't buy the new computer I want because there are too many bills right now... But... I had enough money to pay all the bills!

Maybe your parents won't let you go to a party because there aren't going to be any adults around... But, they'll let you go to another party. Maybe your teachers are giving you tons of homework... But it's almost the end of the school year!

The glass is half full

Take the time to read a section of the Bible from 1 Kings 19... I chose to highlight verse 10, but you should read verses 9-13. In this passage, Elijah might be looking at things from the wrong perspective... He forgets about his job, which is to set the Israelites straight... And thinks about how terrible his life is... They're trying to kill him!

I'm sure you've heard the phrase "Is the glass half empty or half full?" ... Both are correct, but one sounds much better... Right? Perspective makes such a difference in our overall happiness. Choose to see the glass as half full!

I know that sometimes life stinks. It doesn't always go the way we want. It isn't always easy. But try to see things from a positive perspective. You may not be able to change your situation, but you can change the way you deal with it. A change in perspective is the easiest way to make life just a little easier to deal with.

Day 34

> Do not be carried away by all kids of strange teachings.
> (Hebrews 13:9a)

Frisbee Golf

When I play Frisbee there are going to be windows broken, parked cars are in danger... And Frisbees are going to end up on the roof. That's just the way it is.

One day I was playing Frisbee golf with my 3rd - 5th graders. If you aren't familiar with this game, think golf, with Frisbees (wow! you never could have guessed that!)... Each player or team has to throw the disc toward a target and the one with the least amount of throws to hit the target wins that hole.

The wind was blowing, and my throws didn't go straight. It was terrible. Usually they go fairly straight and pretty far... Maybe not in the right direction... But that's a different story... This particular day, they were all over. The wind was making the Frisbee curve funny and sometimes they would go WAY to far, sometimes not far at all.

Christianity is straight and true

Over the years there have been a lot of "fad religions". What I mean is, religions that are popular for a while, then disappear. There have been lots of these, but more recently, maybe you've heard of "Scientology" and "New Age"...

These religions are very popular right now, but in truth, they're like the way I play Frisbee. Their teachings just don't fly straight with what the Bible says. They contradict the Bible, and if you ever have a chance to listen to some "expert" on them speak, they fly all over the place and can't give a straight answer.

The verse in Hebrews talks about not getting caught up with and believing in these false teachings. Stick to learning from what you know is true. The Bible. Ask God today to help you avoid these "fad religions" and follow His word...

Day 35

 For this reason, when I could stand it no longer, I sent to find out about your faith. I was afraid that in some way the tempter might have tempted you and our efforts might have been useless. 1 Thessalonians 3:5

Sniffles

I turned on my computer this morning, opened e-mail and saw the dreaded message: This file contains a virus. My computer had the sniffles. It was going to start acting funny, maybe doing things that I didn't want it to... All because of a virus.

After the proper amount of worry over when it may have been infected, and what it might have done without my consent, I began to think about the proper action to take. Disconnect my computer from the Internet and run anti-virus software.

Fortunately, that seemed to clear up my computer virus. Now I could go on with my day, using my computer and the Internet without worrying about what might happen. Then I took precautions to make sure I didn't have the same problem again. I went and got a firewall program and decided to purchase up-to-date anti-virus software.

Satan is a virus

Paul is writing to the Thessalonians in this verse. Checking up on them to make sure Satan (the tempter) didn't wiggle his way back in to their lives and cause them to fall away from their faith.

I feel like these people in Thessalonica had a "virus" ... Satan is our virus today too. In a very real way, Satan tries to get into our lives and tempt us, get us to question our faith and our God... He sneaks up on us when we're down or when we're weak.

But you know something? We have the best anti-virus and firewall. We can ask God for help, and he's always there protecting us from Satan. Be aware that Satan is real and powerful, but be confident that God is more powerful. Ask God today to help keep you safe from Satan and from giving in to temptation.

Day 36

> As Jesus went on from there, two blind men followed him, calling out, "Have mercy on us, Son of David!" Then he touched their eyes and said, "According to your faith will it be done to you"; and their sight was restored.
> Matthew 9:27, 29-30a

Variety Show

Have you seen the "Nick and Jessica Variety Hour" on TV? They sang, they danced, did skits, changed costumes... All the things variety shows are supposed to have. It was pretty good!

I'm old... So I couldn't help but remember the older variety shows, when special guests used to do magic tricks and illusions and stuff to make the audience think they saw something they didn't. I might have missed it in the Nick and Jessica show, but I didn't see any of that this time.

I started thinking about being young and thinking everything I saw on TV was true... They really were sawing a woman in half or making her disappear... As I got older, I started to know better... But that hasn't stopped people from doing magic tricks... I'm just skeptical now... I don't believe everything I see.

Miracles did happen!

All through Jesus' time here on earth, he performed miracles. Like healing the two blind men, or bringing the little girl back to life. Making wine out of water, feeding five thousand with only a small amount of food... Now those things are really amazing...

But if I was there, would I have been skeptical? Would I have thought this Jesus guy was doing illusions or trying to fool me? Some of the people that were there thought so... They thought he was a demon.

Jesus was an amazing guy. He performed all these miracles, and didn't do it for ratings, or to sell more advertising... He did it because people questioned his authenticity... And he proved he was for real... Over and over again. There was no way to question his authority then... And there's no way to question it now. He's the real thing!

Day 37

 The earth is the Lord's, and everything in it, the world, and all who live in it. Psalm 24:1

Be Careful

A friend was driving me to the store... Weaving in and out of traffic, taking off really fast. When we were looking for a place to park, there was a spot close to the door, but it had shopping carts in the way. I started to get out to move them, but he just pulled in and started pushing them out of the way with the car... "Don't worry... It's a rental"...

A rental car... Which meant it wasn't his, so he didn't care if it was dented and scratched. Would he do that with his own car? Not a chance. His own car gets parked away from everyone so it doesn't get damaged. It gets parked in the garage every night and washed once a week. He takes very good care of his own car.

I guess everyone is kind of like this. We take care of our own stuff better than someone else's. I guess I don't understand though... I try to take care of everyone's stuff... It's a respect thing with me. I wouldn't want anyone to break my things, why would they?

Is it really ours anyway?

Without exception, everything we have is God's. It was all bought with money that was earned because of abilities God gave us. If Psalm 24 is right, and it is... Everything and everyone belongs to God.

So... If everything belongs to God, it's our job to take care of it. The "It isn't mine so I don't have to take care of it" doesn't apply to Christians. We have to think, "Because God owns everything, we have to take care of it the best we can".

The next time you borrow something, a CD, book, clothes... whatever... And you're tempted to do something that could damage it, remember it really belongs to God and you need to take special care of it.

Day 38

> So I find this law at work: When I want to do good, evil is right there with me. For in my inner being I delight in God's law; but I see another law at work in the members of my body, waging war against the law of my mind and making me a prisoner of the law of sin at work within my members.
>
> Romans 7:21-23

Little Voices

Should I eat an Egg McMuffin or shouldn't I? "Well, you are hungry... But you shouldn't spend the money... But it's payday, what's $3... You're trying to diet... One little sandwich, the last one ever... There isn't enough time... Drive thru!" So goes the war of little voices in my head.

Have you ever gone through these battles with yourself? In cartoons they sometimes put the little devil on one shoulder and the angel on the other and the two argue about what to do...

One voice telling you the right thing to do, the other voice convincing you that it's OK to do what you want. I have this every day with things, and I bet you do too. It could be something like whether or not to eat something, or it could be whether to cheat on a test or steal something from a store.

Let the battle begin!

Who knew that those little voices shown in cartoons are really present? Paul was telling the Christians in Rome that there are two parts to us. Our physical bodies and our inner selves. The physical part of us wants immediate satisfaction... For example, "I want an Egg McMuffin." The inner self wants to connect us with what's good.

It's a constant battle for the two voices. It's our nature to want things that may not be the best for us, and it's hard to listen to the voice that tries to convince us to do what's right. Believe me, I know... I eat Egg McMuffins more often than I should.

I pray every day that I'll listen to the voice that tells me the right thing to do, and I pray that for you too... That you'll have the strength to do what's right. Be strong! When the war between the two voices is going on, pray that God will give you the strength to make the right decision.

Day 39

 I know your deeds. See I have placed before you an open door that no one can shut. I know that you have little strength, yet you have kept my word and have not denied my name. Revelation 3:8

Knock, Knock

You can't turn on the television, radio, Internet... Any form of media today and escape the "Reality TV" craze... Whether it's contestants trying to get a job, win money, get a music or modeling contract, a husband or wife... Everyone is talking about "Reality TV".

Personally, I haven't quite figured out why this is so appealing to people, maybe you can explain it to me... But millions of people every day are tuning in to watch people live "regular life" on television...

Of course, without contestants there is no show, and as hard as it is for me to figure out why people want to watch this stuff, it's even harder for me to figure out why people would sign up to be on the shows themselves... But they do... By the thousands, people are going to casting calls, sending in applications... Waiting for their big break... The opportunity of a lifetime!

Real opportunity is not found on TV

I guess I can understand trying to get on these shows... I don't think I would do it, but I think the common theme of these people is that they're all looking for their big break. They're looking for lots of money, fame, attention... And doors to these opportunities may only come once in a lifetime!

In Revelation, John talks about opportunity. God opens a door to eternal life and doesn't close it! Now that's opportunity! He reminds us that we're weak, but that as Christians we try to keep God's word and because of that the door stays open and nobody can close it!

You know, there really aren't that many opportunities that bring fame and fortune... They're out there, but few and far between for most of us... Grab on to the opportunity that God has for you and don't let go! Walk through the open door and in to eternal life.

Day 40

> All the counsel you have received has only worn you out! Let your astrologers come forward, those stargazers who make predictions month by month, let them save you from what is coming upon you. Isaiah 47:13

Signs

What's your sign? What's your birth-date? What are your favorite numbers? What's in your future? What do the stars hold for you? How about "the cards" what do they say? Absolutely nothing. All of it. Astrology is worthless.

It's amazing. People believe this stuff! I don't understand why, but they do. I read these horoscopes in newspapers, in magazines... They're so vague and general you can read anything in to them. Today say hello to someone, they may be special... Well, duh!

These "psychics" advertise on television, in magazines, they have huge signs on their buildings... What I want to know is, if they're really psychic, can they tell when I ride by and think to myself, "That's really stupid"? But, there must be enough people who believe this stuff, or they wouldn't stay in business.

You want a sign?

Even the people in Babylon wanted supernatural help. Do some reading today in Isaiah 47 and you can see that they were trying to get answers from "psychics"... But they didn't have any luck either. Isaiah told the people that even the "psychics" would face God's wrath and couldn't save them...

So why do you think so many people believe in "psychic" powers today? I happen to think it's because people want quick answers. We want to know what the future has in store for us and we don't have the patience (or believe in) God's plan for us...

So... You want a sign? Want to know how to make a decision? Don't believe in astrology or "psychics"... Pray to God. Pray that he'll help you make the right decision, and help you live according to his plan for your life.

Day 41

 The apostles left the Sanhedrin, rejoicing because they had been counted worthy of suffering disgrace for the Name. Day after day, in the temple courts and from house to house, they never stopped teaching and proclaiming the good news that Jesus is the Christ. Acts 5:41-42

Enthusiasm

You really have to be devoted to your cause to be willing to get beat up, picked on, or even die for it. People with that kind of devotion to a cause show a tremendous amount of enthusiasm, don't you think?

Sometimes people that display such devotion to their cause are called martyrs. I bet you can find tons of people who were considered martyrs if you look through a history book. Those people who cared so much for what they believed in that they didn't care about the problems they might face.

I'm sure you've been hearing about all the problems in the Middle East. People killing themselves (and others) with bombs... Obviously we can't agree with what they're doing, or what they believe in. But do you think they're martyrs? Do you think that's why they do these things?

Show some enthusiasm!

Read Acts 5. The apostles were imprisoned, they were beaten and released and told to never teach people about Christianity... And in the verses above, they actually rejoice that they were able to suffer for what they believed in. AND they went right out and told everyone they could about Jesus.

Now that's what I call devotion and enthusiasm... Hopefully you'll never be harmed for talking about what you believe in. But if the apostles were this excited about telling people about Jesus... And they knew there were penalties for doing so, what excuse do we have to not tell everyone about what we know?

Now... I know you'll use some common sense here... Don't put yourself or anyone else in harms way... But be vocal! Be enthusiastic! Tell everyone you know about Jesus. Help your family and friends connect with other people who are Christians. Get them to church, find them a Bible... Do everything you can to spread the word!

Day 42

> Therefore, if anyone is in Christ, he is a new creation; the old has gone, the new has come! 2 Corinthians 5:17

The New You

A young woman wrote to me the other day. She was very excited to tell me that she had become a Christian. She continued on to tell me that she is very confused about the whole thing. She was waiting for this great change... And it didn't happen.

I think that what she was really asking me was... How does Jesus change my life? I accepted Jesus as my Savior, opened my heart to Him... Where is the big change in my every day life?

I don't know where you are in your faith. I don't know where you are in your relationship with God... But maybe, like this young woman, and like me ... and lots of other people I know, you're asking yourself the very same thing. How is Jesus changing my life?

It's a miracle!

Sometimes I wish things would work like they did in the Bible. For example, in Acts, Saul was threatening all the Christians. Jesus appeared to him and made him blind. Then sent a disciple to restore Saul's sight and baptize him as a new Christian.

Wouldn't it be great if things like that happened? OK, I'm a Christian... Help me get A's, heal my friends and family, help with whatever situation I need help with... But it doesn't always work like that.

Our verse today from 2 Corinthians tells us that when we accept Jesus, the old is gone, the new comes... That doesn't necessarily mean that our lives physically change... It means we'll begin to look at things differently. We'll realize that everything is because of God. When we're Christians, God gives us the desire to do what's right and the power to do it!

{ Blessed are the meek, for they will inherit the earth.
Matthew 5:5 }

Conflicting Messages

Climb the corporate ladder, get ahead, be aggressive, win at all costs, answer every question so the teacher thinks about you all the time... Everywhere we turn, the message we hear is the same... You have to stand out from the crowd to get the recognition you deserve.

I'm gonna show you how old I am now. Last night, when I couldn't sleep, I was watching the movie Karate Kid on TV. The idea of the movie is this kid enters a karate contest, and it looks like he's going to win, so the "coach" of the other team tells one of his guys to hurt the Karate Kid so he can't continue.

Daniel, the Karate Kid, is a very quiet kid, he just goes about his business and trains quietly, doesn't look for trouble... He's very humble and quiet. Even when he gets hurt, he doesn't blow up or try to cheat, he crawls back in the ring and quietly wins the competition.

How do you get ahead?

I can think of a lot of examples of humble people who find long-term success. The professional athletes from years ago were much more humble than the ones today. Those are the men and women you here about years after they played and sometimes long after they died!

We live in a world where we're constantly told that you have to do certain things to stand out from the crowd and be remembered or recognized. Matthew tells us that it's not the people that are loud and flashy that have long-term success and recognition, it's the meek, who go about their lives quietly and make a real difference who "inherit the earth".

I'm not suggesting you stop being competitive or giving 100% to everything you do... I'm telling you to leave your ego at home and quietly make a difference in the lives of people who observe you.

Day 44

> And let us consider how we may spur one another on toward love and good deeds. Let us not give up meeting together, as some are in the habit of doing, but let us encourage one another -- and all the more as you see the Day approaching.
> Hebrews 10:24-25

Social Gathering

A while back, when I was visiting family in Michigan I took the time to drive around and see how the town had changed. A lot of the old churches had gone away, the big churches had gotten bigger and there were lots of tiny churches just starting out.

I actually went to one of the "Mega-churches" to look around and see what made them so popular. I got the grand tour of their "campus" and was amazed! They had high tech gadgets, beautiful classrooms and something for every age and every interest.

It was amazing. Christianity in this little town is growing! HUGE numbers of people are going to this church and a couple others like it. But... If these churches have everything, why are there so many small new churches?

Know your role

Today's verse in Hebrews made me think more about that experience. Going to church is so important. Being around other believers is amazing! Church is about more than sitting, singing and listening to a sermon. It's about building believers up and encouraging them.

Think about that for a second. What you come up with might be the answer to my question about "Why all the small churches?" If church is a social event where everyone goes to see people they don't see every day, it's not really the kind of fellowship that Hebrew's is talking about.

If I had to guess, I'd say these small churches are starting because those people feel like church is more of a social event than a time of worship. Think about your role in church. Why you go? To see friends? Talk about what you're going to do the rest of the day or week? Or do you go to be part of a group of believers who build each other up in faith?

Day 45

 May the God of peace, who through the blood of the eternal covenant brought back from the dead our Lord Jesus, that great Shepherd of the sheep, equip you with everything good for doing his will, and may he work in us what is pleasing to him, through Jesus Christ, to whom be the glory for ever and ever. Amen. Hebrews 13:20-21

Toolbox

I remember the day my computer broke. I know quite a bit about computers, so I thought I'd just take off the cover and fix what was broken. I went to find a screwdriver and unplugged the computer only to find out that I need a "Torx" screwdriver.

I was stuck. Even if I had been able to figure out what was wrong with the computer, I couldn't even get to that point, because I didn't have the right tool to get the cover off. I have this with a lot of situations... Maybe you do too.

If you're going to build something, you'll need a saw, hammer, ruler and a bunch of other stuff. If you're going to fix a car, you'll need wrenches and sockets... Painting a room (or a picture)? Guess what... You'll need tools for that too...

The right tools for the job

As Christians, we have responsibilities too. We're told to live a certain way, tell people about Jesus, do things to help others and show our love for others... We have lots of jobs to do!

Pretty scary, huh? We have all these jobs to do and we need tools to do them... Fortunately, we have all the tools we need. We have a great toolbox full of stuff to help us... The Bible, prayer, gifts and talents, good people around us at church, a positive attitude... These are all tools that God put in our toolbox to do His work!

Make sure you make good use of the tools in your tool box ... We were all made with a specific set of tools that help us do exactly what we were put on earth to do... It amazes me to think that God knew exactly what we'd need to do our jobs ... and gave us the tools to do it... Now it's up to us to use those tools to the best of our abilities.

Day 46

> For I am convinced that neither death nor life, neither angels nor demons, neither the present nor the future, nor any powers, neither height nor depth, nor anything else in all creation, will be able to separate us from the love of God that is in Christ Jesus our Lord. Romans 8:38-39

Disconnected

When I had technical problems with my new computer it had to be serviced, and I was computer-less! I never stopped to think about how much of my days are spent thinking about the young people in my life, how much time I spend clicking around the internet, and how much my world revolves around getting information like news and weather online... I was completely disconnected!

A whole week where e-mail was piling up, I couldn't chat with anyone, couldn't find resources to get things done... It was driving me crazy! It's a little scary to realize how dependant you are on a computer on a daily basis.

How dependent are you on technology? How often do you check e-mail, chat with your friends, look stuff up, read the news, play games... If you're like me, without it you would feel completely separate from the rest of the world!

Nothing can separate us

In Romans, Paul is telling the church in Rome, and us, that no matter what happens, we always have the love of Jesus. No matter what happens, we can always remember that Jesus is with us. No matter how bad things are or what we do, we always have that love.

Sometimes we feel disconnected from the rest of the world. Maybe our computers break, or we're busy, on vacation... Or other stuff that keeps you from talking to friends or doing the things you enjoy. You feel like you're on another planet! But no matter what comes along, we'll never be separated from the love of Jesus.

Now that is good news... When I was thinking about all the stuff I was missing all week, I just kept thinking about that... That Jesus loves me, and is with you too... Suddenly I didn't feel so disconnected... I hope you're able to remember that the next time you feel separated from the world.

Day 47

 Remember how the Lord your God led you all the way in the desert these forty years, to humble you and to test you in order to know what was in your heart, whether or not you would keep his commands. Deuteronomy 8:2

Leap Of Faith

I was watching the movie Renaissance Man. It's an older movie, but one of my favorites. In one of the scenes, Bill, a civilian teacher climbs the victory tower and has to get down. His students tell him to put his feet down over the edge and find the ledge to stand on. He can't see it, and at first can't feel it... But he has to have enough trust in his students to believe it's there.

I've been in a lot of situations that required me to have faith. For example, how I started working for the church: I lost my job and couldn't find another one. There were days in the past when I've wondered about where I was going to get the money to do something... I had to have faith that if I built a website, people would find it...

The list goes on and on... There have been lots of times where I had to take a leap of faith. I'm sure you've been in situations like that too. Maybe you or someone you know has health problems, or relationship problems, or job problems... You may find yourself asking why... "Why does this have to happen to me?!"

Faith tested

In the Bible, there are lots of times when people had to have extreme faith. Think Noah. "Hello, Noah. This is God. I know you live miles away from lakes and oceans, and you've never seen rain... But build an ark because there's going to be a flood." Or how about today's verse... God led his people through the dessert for 40 years! Even though they complained, they had faith.

It's hard to have faith that things happen for a reason. But you know what? God has a plan... And we're part of it. Have faith that everything happens for a reason and that God is in control of everything.

Bad stuff happens... Sometimes to good people. It's a fact of life. Sometimes we aren't sure why these things happen. Sometimes we don't understand. Sometimes it feels like we just can't take any more... Have faith, my friend, everything will be OK.

Day 48

> All this happened to us, though we had not forgotten you or been false to your covenant. Our hearts had not turned back; our feet had not strayed from your path.
> Psalm 44:17-18

Remember Me?

I once had a rough week. My computer was in the shop, I had car problems, was really busy doing work stuff, Maggie (my loving lil puppy) was sick... All this stuff happened... And I had to cancel meetings and youth group events... I was worried that the kids at church would forget about me!

Lately, it just seems like things haven't gone exactly the way I planned. Things have gotten messed up, misplaced, or just not worked out right... Ever feel like that happens to you?

No matter what you do... How hard you work, how much you try to do the right thing, how you plan and schedule, how you think things through... Sometimes things just don't go your way...

Real despair

Do you know what despair means? It means: to give up all hope. When things don't go my way, sometimes that's how I feel. But you know what? When I feel that way I read Psalm 44 yesterday... When you're feeling this way you should too!

Psalm 44 talks all about the terrible things that have happened. They got beat in battle, spread apart... All the other nations were laughing at them! Obviously this was not in their plan... The author cries out, asking why God has forgotten them and let all these things happen.

Sometimes I feel the same way... I'm sure you do too... We try to do the right things, but sometimes it just feels like God forgets us... Reading Psalm 44 made me realize that my problems aren't really so big... And I'm not alone... Even thousands of years ago people thought this way... But God didn't forget them, and he doesn't forget us.

Day 49

 Then Paul, knowing that some of them were Sadducees and the others Pharisees, called out in the Sanhedrin, "My brothers, I am a Pharisee, the son of a Pharisee. I stand on trial because of my hope in the resurrection of the dead." When he said this, a dispute broke out between the Pharisees and the Sadducees, and the assembly was divided.

Acts 23:6-7

Trouble Makers

When I was a kid, I used to "play both ends against the middle." For example, I'd tell my mom that my dad said one thing, and tell my dad that mom said something so that I could get what I wanted... It didn't ever work because they were too smart to fall for that.

Have you ever tried that? I bet you have... With parents, friends, teachers... I think we all have done that at one time or another... We always try it when we're trying to get something we want or get our way with a certain situation, or maybe we do it when we're trying to get out of trouble...

Sometimes that behavior could be called "Stirring the pot"... Whatever you call it, you've likely had people try to do it to you as well. I've also seen people try to cause a disturbance and shift the focus off of them... Same kind of idea...

Is it OK to "Stir the pot?"

In this particular verse of Acts, Paul is being confronted by a group of people. In order to save himself, Paul told the group, who he knew was divided on some issues, that he was a Pharisee who believed in resurrection...

Guess what... Paul was 'Stirring the pot" and he got the two groups, the Pharisees and Sadducees to argue about who was right and who was wrong... They were so busy fighting, the commander took Paul away so he wouldn't get hurt. Pretty good thinking on his part, don't you think?

The point is, there are some times when playing both ends against each other is OK. When two groups of people who are out to get us start arguing against each other, and their goal is to keep us from doing right, getting them to disagree on something is easy because their arguments against us are weak.

Day 50

> The five men who had spied out the land went inside and took the carved image, the ephod, the other household gods and the cast idol while the priest and the six hundred armed men stood at the entrance to the gate. Judges 18:17

Black Cats

In my life, I've known people who were afraid of black cats, broken mirrors and walking under ladders because all of those things bring bad luck. I've also known people who had charms and dolls because they brought good luck.

All these things are superstitions. It's amazing to me that people really believe some of these things... "Step on a crack, break your mothers back" ... Baseball players who won't step on the white lines because it's bad luck... Athletes who wear the same socks every game... The list goes on and on.

Superstitions are funny things... Sometimes they just get passed down through generations as stories. It's hard to know where they come from, but lots of people, probably someone you know, believes in one or more of these things... Or maybe one of a million other superstitions!

Good luck and bad luck

I guess I never paid much attention to superstitions. I was never afraid of any of those things and I always wondered where they started... People who believe in these things really place power in mirrors, and cats, and whatever else... These things rule their lives and scare them or maybe bring false hope in some cases.

As you probably know, I spend time every day reading and thinking about passages in the Bible. In Judges 18, people went crazy to get all the false gods and idols and stuff. They thought this great land that they were taking over in battle was so good because of these idols!

They were superstitious too! They were placing false power in these gods. They thought they would be kept safe and be blessed because the people who had them before were. So maybe that's where superstitions started... I don't know for sure... But what I do know is that we need to put all our faith in the one true God... That's where all our blessings come from.

Day 51

> Then will I go to the altar of God, to God, my joy and my delight. I will praise you with the harp, O God, my God.
> Psalm 43:4

Let's Make A Deal

How many times have you tried to make a deal with someone? "Will you take me to a movie if I clean my room? How about if I clean my room and do the dishes for a week?" or maybe, "Could you loan me $5 until next week so I can buy lunch? I'll pay you back $10 and buy you lunch on Monday."

I bet you probably try to make deals all the time. I know I do. Maybe it started when you were young and agreed to do things to get a toy. As you get older, the deals got tougher... You agree to take out the garbage and vacuum the house if you're able to stay out later...

What makes a deal good is when both people involved get some benefit from it. Thinking back, the deals that my parents took me up on were ones that let me stay up or out later but got work around the house done. They always passed on the deals that only helped me.

Deals in the Old Testament

There were a lot of "deals" made in the Old Testament, but they weren't all good deals. A lot of them benefited only the people, not God. The deals were hard to keep because some of them were made when people were really scared or in trouble.

In the example from Psalm 43, the deal is, "Keep me safe from wicked people... And I will praise you with a harp." Shouldn't that happen anyway? This is a deal that benefits God indirectly... Because He is being praised... But... He should be praised anyway, that seems like a hollow deal to me... How about you?

Try not to get caught up in making deals with God when times are tough or you're scared. They are often hard to follow through with because once God keeps his end of the deal, we may forget ours. Making a deal like, "God, if you let me win this game, I'll..." Is a hard deal to keep. Praise God in everything you do, and be careful when you're making a "deal".

Day 52

{ But Ruth replied, "Don't urge me to leave you or to turn back from you. Where you go I will go, and where you stay I will stay. Your people will be my people and your God my God. Where you die I will die, and there I will be buried. May the Lord deal with me, be it ever so severely, if anything but death separates you and me." Ruth 1:16-17 }

Buddy List

Friends come and go. I haven't talked to some of my best friends from school in over 10 years! There are friends I see once in a while, people I met at work or through other events that I did a lot with for a while, and don't see them any more.

Sometimes there are friends that we keep forever. Some we stay in touch with but aren't as close. Interests change, families change, sometimes people move, sometimes there are just silly things that force us to stop being friends with people.

Now, with the Internet, we have instant messenger. Almost everyone has a screen name now. We meet people in chat rooms, on message boards, playing games... All these people are friends and they all get on our buddy lists.

Real friends

I bet you have a lot of friends too. Probably from school, maybe church, maybe some Internet friends. But, it's important to know who your really good friends are... Those are the people who stick with you through good and bad things. Not just when things are good.

Read Ruth 1 to learn about real friendship. Ruth was a good friend to Naomi. When both of them lost a loved one, Ruth stayed with Naomi to keep her company. Ruth tells Naomi that no matter what happens, she will be her friend. Now that's someone I want on my buddy list.

Think about all your friends today... Make a list of a few of your very best friends. Write some things that a friend would and wouldn't do. Keep this friendship list and add to it throughout your life. It will help you choose your friends wisely and to treat them well. Good friends are hard to find, but are the best thing in the world to have when you do find them.

Day 53

> There will be no more night. They will not need the light of a lamp or the light of the sun, for the Lord God will give them light. And they will reign forever and ever.
> Romans 22:5

Favorite Things

Rain drops on roses and whiskers on kittens, Bright copper kettles and warm woolen mittens, Brown paper packages tied up with strings, Cream colored ponies and crisp apple strudels, Doorbells and sleigh bells and schnitzel with noodles, Wild geese that fly with the moon on their wings. Maybe you remember this song...

The lines above are from a song in the movie "The Sound of Music"... And the next line is "These are a few of my favorite things." If I made a list of some of my favorite things, they would probably go something like this: Drums, baseball, computers, reading, spending time with the kids at church, cooking... The list could go on forever!

When I think about my favorite things I also think of some Bible verses that really mean something to me, encourage me, give me strength, keep me in line, make my faith stronger... My favorite verses come from all over the Bible and apply to a lot of things in my life.

Making a list of your favorite things is such a great thing to do. Every now and then you need to write down a list of all the things you love... Hobbies, books, television shows, sports teams, Bible verses... Everything you can think of!

Some of my favorites

Don't let anyone look down on you because you are young, but set an example for the believers in speech, in life, in love, in faith and in purity. (1 Timothy 4:12)

Jesus answered, "I am the way and the truth and the life. No one comes to the Father except through me." (John 14:6)

Trust in the Lord with all your heart and lean not on your own understanding; in all your ways acknowledge him, and he will make your paths straight. (Proverbs 3:5-6)

Day 54

> It is good to praise the Lord and make music to your name, O Most High, to proclaim your love in the morning and your faithfulness at night, to the music of the ten-stringed lyre and the melody of the harp. For you make me glad by your deeds, O Lord; I sing for joy at the works of your hands.
>
> Psalm 92:1-4

Cleared For Takeoff

Making airplanes is so much fun. There are so many different kinds to make, some that fly long and straight, some that do tricks. Mine never fly very well, and are often were hazardous to the health of everyone in the neighborhood... They go all over!

I've seen groups make paper airplanes and fly them together... There were all types of planes and flights... There were some smooth flights, some went up down around and all over but still flew a long way, some never made it off the runway because they didn't stay together... And some (like mine) should never leave the runway.

Thinking about paper airplanes and how well (or not!) they fly reminds me of our relationship with God. Sometimes we cruise along smooth and steady, sometimes there are lots of bumps and other turbulence and sometimes we stand still on the runway.

Air Traffic Control

Psalm 92 is really about relationships, I think. Taking time out of every day, to praise God and think about what He has to say in the Bible. Sure, sometimes the ride is bumpy, sometimes we feel like we're flying on our own and sometimes our relationship with God is a smooth flight. But we still have to Praise God every day.

Think for a minute about your relationship with God. Think in terms of airplanes... If your relationship was represented by an airplane, where would you be in your flight? Would you be cruising along safe and sound? Having a bumpy ride? Doing tricks? Or sitting on the runway wondering if you can even fly at all?

Take time to figure out what your flight plan is. What are the big things in your relationship with God? Where do you want to go? What can you do to arrive at your final destination? Just remember... No matter how bumpy the ride, God is your Air Traffic Controller guiding you along the way...

Day 55

 So then, just as you received Christ Jesus as Lord, continue to live in him. Colossians 2:6

Walk The Walk

I came from a good Christian home. I went to church every week, went to Sunday School, went to a Christian school... I learned all about Jesus everywhere I went. I had to memorize Bible verses and really learn all about Christianity and how Jesus died for me...

You know something? All of those things were great. I learned a lot in Sunday School and at church and in regular school. But those things really had very little to do with me being a Christian today. The single, most important reason that I am a Christian today is because of my parents.

It's true! My mom and dad always seemed to do the right thing. They always helped people out, always prayed, always read the Bible, always lived as though everything they did was for the glory of God. He was always the reason for all their actions. The only reason I am who I am now is because I saw two people modeling Christianity.

Live a Christian life

I hope that like me, you have good role models to follow. I hope you go to church, youth group, study the Bible, and pray. But maybe, you are nervous about being a Christian in public or talking to your friends about Jesus. I know I was.

I "caught" Christianity by seeing my parents live a Christian life. Make sure you read that again. All the teaching didn't make me a Christian. It made me smarter. But I became a Christian by watching people live that lifestyle... People around you might "catch" Christianity too.

Colossians tells us to live a Christian life. If you do that, other people will notice. You'll be helping your friends and family catch Christianity. Once they do, you'll be able to encourage them to learn more about that life. Actions speak much louder than words!

Day 56

> Sing for joy to God our strength; shout aloud to the God of Jacob! Begin the music, strike the tambourine, play the melodious harp and lyre. Psalm 81:1-2

Joyful Noise

Growing up in a family who loved music, I remember enjoying all the songs in church, going to special musical programs, concerts, recitals and choir programs and hearing all different styles of music. Some good, some not what I enjoy, but I always remember my mom saying "Oh, well... They're making a joyful noise!"

I can't sing a note. I love music, and when I'm alone, I've been known to sing with lots of enthusiasm. I love songs with energy and a beat I can tap my foot to.

Most people I know enjoy listening to music. How about you? I listen to and love Christian music... But I also listen to all different styles of music, both religious and non-religious. Most people I know listen to a specific type of music without giving thought to anything else. They just like what they like and see no value in any other style.

Music isn't secular or Christian

I hear people of all ages arguing about what good music is. Some people think music with drums is bad... Can you believe it? Drums? Bad?! Some people think rock music or hip-hop or country is terrible. They can't even imagine listening to that trash. You might not like Beethoven or J.S. Bach or other classical music.

I've been listening to an instrumental CD. Most people would consider it rock music. It's amazing! Some Christians might wonder how a Christian could listen to such noise. I don't like death metal or the really obscene and violent rap songs. But it isn't the music that bothers me... Some of those songs have a great beat!

I don't like those songs because of the words. It has nothing to do with the music. Music by itself isn't "Christian" or "non-Christian" it's music. It's the words that put the songs in a particular category. Music is a gift from God... In all forms and styles.

Day 57

 Be strong and let us fight bravely for our people and the cities of our God. The Lord will do what is good in his sight.
2 Samuel 10:12

Love Of Country

Every spring in the United States we celebrate Memorial Day. Sometimes we think of it as the first day of summer. Everyone cooks outside, has picnics, parties, spends time with family and friends, gets a day off from school or work... It's a day to relax!

Lately Memorial Day has been different for me. Maybe it's because I'm getting older (not old... old-er!), maybe it's because Reverend Marsden was a Navy Chaplain and made me more aware of the holiday, maybe it's because I spent a lot of hours packing boxes for troops in Iraq, maybe it's because the war is on my TV every day... Maybe, maybe, maybe...

Whatever the reason, I keep thinking that while I'm enjoying a day to relax and cook outside, there are men and women who are away from their families and friends... They're not cooking hotdogs or swimming or having picnics.

Take a moment

In the past, I never really thought much about war veterans. I looked at Memorial Day like many others do... A holiday from school and work... But with all the stuff going on in the world, it's different.

Somewhere along the way, lots of us forgot how we got to today. Many of us don't really understand and appreciate what the armed forces and the men and women who serve go through.

I once had to interview a veteran. None of the stuff he told me was in a history book, but that didn't mean it wasn't history. I want to challenge you to do two things... Pray for the soldiers who are serving our country now, and for the ones who have served in the past. And second, take time to thank a veteran and learn from them... They helped us arrive at today, and they deserve our thanks and respect.

Day 58

> And the Lord said, "Listen to what the unjust judge says. And will not God bring about justice for his chosen ones, who cry out to him day and night? Will he keep putting them off? I tell you, he will see that they get justice, and quickly."
>
> Luke 18:6-8a

Getting Stuff Done

You know how your parents, teachers, friends, etc. keep reminding you to take care of something? Take out the trash, clean your room, do your homework, help me with... And you figure you'll get around to it eventually, and that person keeps bugging you and driving you crazy reminding you that it needs to get done... Congratulations, you're being nagged.

I don't know about you, but the more I get nagged to do something, the less likely I am to do it. And the more I'm reminded to get it done, the more frustrated I get. I get mad. I get loud. I get quiet. I find something else to do. Whatever my reaction is, it gets worse the more I get nagged.

I'm not sure why people feel the need to nag me. Maybe they think I'll get it done faster. Maybe they think I forgot. Maybe they just have nothing else to think about. Maybe it's a high priority for them. Whatever the case, eventually I get around to the task and the nagging stops... Until the next time I put something off.

It's OK to nag... Sometimes.

In Luke, there's a story about an unjust judge. A woman goes to this judge over and over asking for help. He keeps turning her down. Eventually, he gives in and helps her... Pretty much to keep her from bothering him. Was she a nag? Or persistent?

The point to the story is simple: keep praying. Sometimes it's OK to nag God. The story in Luke promises that God will bring justice to those who pray continually. We get angry for being nagged, God will not. Be persistent!

I think sometimes we give up too easily. Why do you think that is? Maybe it's because we think there's no answer... I don't know why, but I know there are things that I give up on too easily. What kinds of prayers do you think God wants us to be persistent with? Pray faithfully, knowing that God will grant justice to those who are persistent.

Day 59

> So the kinsman-redeemer said to Boaz, "Buy it yourself." And he removed his sandal. Then Boaz announced to the elders and all the people, "Today you are witnesses that I have bought from Naomi all the property of Elimelech, Kilion and Mahlon." Ruth 4:8-9

Cross My Heart

There are ways to "seal a deal". You know, a gesture or phrase that both people agree to that makes the deal strong. "Pinkie swear", "Cross my heart", or maybe a handshake. Whatever it is, it keeps the other person from backing out of a deal.

Why do you think these gestures of good faith are needed? If the deal is good, do we really need to do these gestures? I mean, I know the "Pinkie swear" is a gesture that nobody would break, but if the deal is fair, why should we be concerned that it will be broken?

I guess it's just a matter of good sense. Things happen, people don't always hold their end of the deal, no matter how fair it was in the first place. Maybe the conditions change. For example If I agree to make payments on a car, and it stops running or I'm not happy with it, without some kind of contract, I could just stop paying.

Shake on it

Sometimes movie characters say things like, "You have my word on it" or "My handshake is as good as gold"... Those comments are good faith gestures. Today, people sign contracts so neither side can back out of them.

In the Old Testament when Boaz wanted to buy property, they used a "good faith" gesture too but it wasn't like today. They didn't shake on it, or sign contracts... They removed a sandal. That's how they made the deal official. Pretty wild, huh?

If you're making a deal today, you may not want to take off your shoe as a "good faith" gesture, but just think about something... When did the world stop accepting and respecting a hand shake or promise and start requiring other forms of good faith? Let's see if we can make a difference in the way things work... Let's make good faith gestures, and keep them so that our word is as solid and as much of a promise as signing a contract.

Day 60

> Just as man is destined to die once, and after that to face judgment, so Christ was sacrificed once to take away the sins of many people; and he will appear a second time, not to bear sin, but to bring salvation to those who are waiting for him. Hebrews 9:27-28

The Other Side

After life, the great beyond, flip side, eternal reward... All these things are used to explain what happens after we die. Christians believe one thing... That we go to heaven. Some religions believe that we just die and that's it or that we come back as something else based on how we lived this life.

Through the years, I've had a lot of ideas about what heaven might be like. A huge house... Resort... Clouds... Place where angels fly around... Seem silly to you? Well, what do you think heaven is like? Maybe you have a different picture of heaven than I do...

There are probably as many versions of what heaven is like as there are people. We all have a different picture of what it will be like. Sometimes I think it doesn't matter what heaven is like. It doesn't matter if heaven is a resort or a huge house... It only matters that heaven is real.

Death and taxes

In Hebrews, we learn that Jesus will be coming back and we'll be judged. As believers, we know that even though we're sinners, because Jesus died on a cross, we're forgiven and will go to heaven... But those who aren't Christians face hell...

So today, think about this... How does your belief in the afterlife affect how you live today? Waiting until tomorrow to "do the right thing" or give your life completely to God could be too late! We never know when Jesus will return.

Maybe you've heard something like, "The only things that are guaranteed are death and taxes"... Which means, we're all going to have to pay taxes and we're all going to die eventually. You probably don't think about death much... For most people it's not really a happy subject... But you know what? It's not so bad for me because I believe that I'm going to heaven!

Day 61

 We do not dare to classify or compare ourselves with some who commend themselves. When they measure themselves by themselves and compare themselves with themselves, they are not wise. 2 Corinthians 10:12

The Jones'

Do you know people who are always comparing themselves to others? "They have more friends, more money, nicer clothes..." The comparisons go on and on. They make themselves crazy by comparing what they have (or don't have) to what other people have.

It's easy to do, I guess... We're taught to work hard, be the best, and have the best stuff... But there's a difference, between striving for all these things, and worrying if someone else has bigger, better or more stuff than you do. Don't you think?

Do you find yourself making comparisons to your friends? Why do you think people are so obsessed with what others have? Whether it's things, talents, money or whatever, when we make comparisons, we feel bad. So why do we do it?

Maybe you ARE the Jones'

In 2 Corinthians 10:10-17, Paul is telling us to stop comparing ourselves to others. He's telling us that we should be content with whatever God provides for us. He's telling the people in Corinth to stop worrying about how much they're spreading the Gospel and stop comparing themselves to other nations...

So even way back in the Bible, people were consumed with "Keeping up with the Jones'." It's the same old story, everyone wants to be the best and have the best... What we really need to do is strive to work hard and be the best without comparing our lives to someone else.

In our world there will always someone better, someone with more stuff, someone with just what you want out there. That's why God encourages us not to compare ourselves to others. That's not to say you shouldn't strive to succeed or improve... But it does mean that your identity should be based on God's assessment, not based upon how you measure up to someone else.

Day 62

 A good name is more desirable than great riches; to be esteemed is better than silver or gold. Proverbs 22:1

What's Important?

Isn't it amazing how labels are put on people? Jock, dumb-blonde, nerd, preppy, goth, rich, poor... Some aren't bad, some are just plain mean. All these labels are a description of a persons "reputation" ... Sometimes reputations are earned, sometimes they are rumors, sometimes they are just stuck on a person who's part of a group.

Why do young people work so hard to have (or not have!) a certain reputation? Why are labels so important? I guess It's not only young people who are concerned with reputations and labels.

Take me, for example... I've been labeled "funny" and "unorganized". I've earned these reputations... Most people think I'm funny and everyone who knows me knows I'm not organized, even though I try to be. These are both reputations I've earned.

Your reputation

Reputations are earned by choices we make... either good or bad. Sometimes we build individual reputations, sometimes we're "lumped in" with part of a group. I earned the reputation of "unorganized" all on my own through. As a Christian, sometimes people have labeled me as someone who preaches to everyone and bugs people until they give up and listen. Which isn't true... but I've been labeled as part of a group.

How do labels affect the way you treat someone? Maybe you're more likely to pick on a nerd than a jock. What reputations do you think Christians have in today's world? Do you think we've earned it? Do we need to change it? Can we? How? Maybe if we work on our individual reputations, the world will label the "group" of Christians differently.

Each choice you make affects your reputation. Once you're labeled that reputation is very difficult to change in other people's minds. Think about your personal reputation and how Christians are labeled... If those labels need to be changed start today.

Day 63

 "Surely God does not reject a blameless man or strengthen the hands of evildoers. He will yet fill your mouth with laughter and your lips with shouts of joy." Job 8:20-21

Turn That Frown...

Maybe you've heard the phrase "Turn that frown upside down"... My mom used to say that to me all the time, mostly when I was pouting about something, or if I had gotten a bump and just couldn't stop crying. She figured that I couldn't laugh and cry at the same time, and it was better to listen to a kid laugh than cry...

I think what she was really teaching me is that laughter makes even the worse things seem a little better. Laughing may not fix the problem or make a situation go away, but makes the situation just a little easier to deal with... Don't you think?

I think for that reason I try to stay positive and laugh through rough times. Pouting or crying doesn't help, and laughter can't hurt. Who knows? Maybe laughter puts you in a better place to have something good happen... I mean, if you're pouting and miserable, you're not going to be looking for something good to happen.

A laugh a day

According to Job, laughter is a gift from God... Who knew? I think this is a message telling us that God gives us the ability to laugh through the bad times and we should take full advantage of it...

Now this doesn't mean that it's always appropriate to laugh. I can think of times when it's probably best to be solemn... Like at a funeral... People are there to remember someone who passed away... It's probably a bad idea to laugh in the middle of the service. Can you think of any times that laughter isn't appropriate?

I guess the point of all this is that sometimes laughter is the only thing that gets us through a rough situation. God promises an abundant life, but that doesn't mean a stress and sorrow-free life. God gave us emotions and wants us to use and enjoy them all... Including laughter!

Day 64

> But you, man of God, flee from all this, and pursue righteousness, godliness, faith, love, endurance and gentleness. Fight the good fight of the faith. Take hold of the eternal life to which you were called when you made your confession in the presence of many witnesses.
> 1 Timothy 6:11-12

Drive To Succeed

Over the years, there have been lots of things that I worked really hard at. My drive to be successful doesn't allow for doing things half way. If I'm going to do something, I'm going to be good at it... And if I have to work really hard to make that happen, that's just the way it is.

Maybe you have the same desire to succeed as I do. Maybe you wanted to learn how to play an instrument (the drums perhaps?) or be good at a sport, or be a good student... You probably had to work really hard to be as good as you wanted.

When I wanted to be good at baseball, I practiced for hours every day. When I wanted to learn how to play the drums, I practiced and practiced (even though you'd never know it!) and now in my job at Old Paramus I work very hard to come up with good ideas for the youth groups.

If you spent

So, I asked myself a question, and now I'm going to ask you the same... If you spent half as much time working on your relationship with God as you do with practicing (or whatever you work hard at), what would your relationship be like?

I think of practicing (and all the other things we work at) as a discipline. Now, that does not mean punishment, although I know it's the same word... Discipline can also mean training... And in addition to the training like we thought of before, there are also spiritual disciplines... Things like reading the Bible, praying, quiet time to study and reflect...

Even though faith in Christ justifies us before God, it doesn't mean we can relax and coast through life without a relationship with God. Make the decision to work on your spiritual disciplines, add Bible time and prayer time to your schedule and stay motivated to practice those as much as you do the other disciplines in your life.

Day 65

 Do not store up for yourselves treasures on earth, where moth and rust destroy, and where thieves break in and steal. But store up for yourselves treasures in heaven, where moth and rust do not break in and steal. For where your treasure is, there your heart will be also. Matthew 6:19-21

Sparkle And Fade

The world today is consumed with "Bigger, better, faster" things. I'm as guilty as anyone of this... I wanted a new computer because my old one wasn't working right... I could have gotten a less expensive one, but I wanted the latest greatest model.

The whole world seems to be like this... Think back to things that seemed so important... Games, instruments... Whatever. They get used for a while... Until the next "had to have" thing comes. It's different from "keeping up with the Jones'"; it's a matter of wanting the latest, greatest, newest... Stuff.

The things that are so important and great in our lives are quickly "yesterdays news" when we find the next thing we want... We're almost like my dog... She can't focus on one thing for 30 seconds before she's on to the next toy...

Used today, forgotten tomorrow

I know of groups that play a game called bigger, better. Go through the neighborhood, show people an object and ask if they can give something bigger and better. I'm not saying this is a bad thing... But, it all feeds in to the "gotta have the latest greatest" lifestyle we're all right in the middle of.

Jesus gave us this incredible lesson in Matthew 6. He said that all the things we want in life are only good here, but don't give us everlasting life. Sometimes I think we put too much importance on "stuff" and forget that all those things don't really help us in the long run. All the things I wanted really, really bad were great for a while, but before long end up in a pile with the rest of the stuff I never use.

I'm not telling you that you should give up everything or that you shouldn't "want stuff" because there are some things we all need... Clothes, food, shelter, etc. It's not even bad to want "luxury" items... But just remember that your life should not revolve around those things...

Day 66

> The people expected him (Paul) to swell up or suddenly fall dead, but after waiting a long time and seeing nothing unusual happen to him, they changed their minds and said he was a god. Acts 28:6

I Wanna Go Too!

I've been known to change my mind. There's a story my sister tells about this. The short version is... She would ask if I wanted to go along somewhere, and I would say no. Then scream as loud as I could, as they were driving down the driveway, that I did wanted to go... But when they came to get me...I really didn't want to go along.

I wish I could say that this "changing my mind" thing stopped when I turned five... But, to this day, one minute to the next I change... Ask me now and I may not want to do something... But again in 2 minutes and I might change my mind.

I think most people change their minds... Maybe it's just part of being human. Most of the time it's harmless... Annoying but not really bad.

Make up your mind!

It's the things that aren't very important that I change my mind about... Whether or not to get dessert, whether or not to go for a walk... The things that are important to me... Religion, for example... I don't change my mind about. Maybe it's the same with everyone. If you really believe in something, you aren't likely to change your mind. Sometimes people who change their minds about important things do so because they haven't studied the issue.

It's kinda like the story of Paul in Acts... He gets bitten by a poisonous snake and the people think he's going to die... When he doesn't they change their tune from "He's an evil person" to "he's a god!" These people were ignorant because they "believed" one thing, but when that seemed wrong, they changed their minds completely!

In our own lives, we have to be careful to study carefully and really believe in what we're saying because if we change our views on Christianity every five minutes, what does that say to the people who are watching and listening? That we don't know what we're talking about...

Day 67

 He said, "This is what the king who will reign over you will do: He will take your sons and make them serve with his chariots and horses, and they will run in front of his chariots...When that day comes, you will cry out for relief from the king you have chosen, and the Lord will not answer you in that day." 1 Samuel 8:11,18

Told Ya So

Have you ever had an "I told you so" moment? That's when someone warned you about something, you ignored their warning, went ahead with the action or plan and just like that person said, something happened... They were right, and you get an, "I told you so."

Sometimes it's parents, teachers, or friends who give you advice that you ignore. I've had it more times than I can even count... People have told me to plan things better, or do things differently... And when they don't work out like I planned, I get the big, "I told you so".

Maybe it's because we don't like to be told what to do... Maybe it's because we're too proud to except that someone else had a better idea or way of doing something, because we think we know everything, or because we think we can get away with doing it our way... But, I'm sure that like me, you've had an "I told you so" moment.

We always know better

Take a few minutes to read 1 Samuel 8. Samuel tells the people that a king is going to treat them badly. There's a whole list of things that a king will do. He tries to remind them they have God and don't need a king. He warns them. But do they listen?

No. They know better. All the other nations have kings and they want one too. They need a great warrior to keep them safe and provide for them. They want a king. Period. And nothing anyone tells them is going to make a difference.

Eventually all the stuff bad stuff happens, and it was an "I told you so" moment. So, listen carefully to all the advice people give you... That doesn't mean you have to follow it all, but every bit of information you can have to help you make a decision is going to help you make the right one... And hopefully avoid an "I told you so".

Day 68

> The tribes of Israel sent men throughout the tribe of Benjamin, saying, "What about this awful crime that was committed among you? Now surrender those wicked men of Gibeah so that we may put them to death and purge the evil from Israel." But the Benjamites would not listen to their fellow Israelites. Judges 20:12-13

All Those In Favor

When I was younger I remember times when I got in trouble for just knowing about something... One of those times, I must have been around 12 and my neighbor and friend at the time was maybe 9 or 10... He was going to an empty field to light fireworks... I knew he was going, but decided not to join him.

When he got in trouble, I got in trouble for not stopping him or telling an adult that he was going to do this... Now, let me ask you... Does that sound fair to you? It sure didn't to me, but that was the way it went anyway. I had agreed that his actions were OK because I didn't stop him.

This kind of thing happens all the time! People get in trouble for "looking the other way". Have you ever done that or know someone who has? Leaving when someone was going to steal something, or the lookout while friends were smoking...

Keeping silent is silently agreeing

In Judges there's a story about how one of the tribes of Israel murdered someone. When everyone figured out what happened, they decided to punish the people that did the crime. They got a group together and went to get the bad guys.

This group of Israelites asked the tribe of Benjamin to bring out the bad guys, but they refused! Since they didn't help they were saying the crime wasn't so bad. In the end, the people of the tribe of Benjamin were destroyed in battle.

Just remember that you can be held accountable for others peoples actions, even if you weren't really involved. These are situations where it's hard to stand up for what you agree with and stop people from doing things... It's even harder to go to an adult and talk to them about what might happen. But in the end, it's really preventing something bad from happening.

Day 69

 "I am about to go the way of all the earth," he said. "So be strong, show yourself a man, and observe what the Lord your God requires: Walk in his ways, and keep his decrees and commands, his laws and requirements." 1 Kings 2:2-3

I Love You, Dad

Sometimes I think about all the good times I had with my dad over the years. All the happy memories, all the wisdom he shared with me, all the instruction he gave me... After all, what kind of son would I be if I didn't reflect on the life of my dad once in a while?

I couldn't even begin to share with you all the wisdom my dad shared with me through the years. I can't teach you everything he taught me. But... I'm gonna try. Read on though... There is a point... Not just fond memories of my personal hero.

My dad was really a handy guy. Mr. Fixit. He tried SO hard to teach me all these things, but thankfully for him, he had a son-in-law who grasped the Mr. Fixit stuff better than me... Wow, all the stories I could tell about Mr. Fixit...

That's why you use a rubber handled screwdriver!

There were lots of times when his lessons really sunk in, but none more than when Mr. Fixit was working with electricity. "Now, boys... Remember to turn off all the electricity when you're working with these wires," says my dad...

As my dad started poking his screwdriver around, he got the shock of his life when the metal touched wires that still had electricity running through them at which point he jumped 10 feet in the air and exclaimed, "Now THAT'S why you use a rubber handled screwdriver!" The real lesson wasn't "be sure to turn off the power" it was, rubber handles keep you from getting such a big shock that it kills ya.

In the verse today, David gives his son, Solomon the best lesson ever. Dads all have information that is important for us to learn. Make sure you spend time with your dad so he can teach ya all the lessons. Dads are pretty smart guys. Make sure you tell yours how much you love him not just by words, but also by spending time with him and including him in your activities. You'll learn more from your dad than anyone...

Day 70

> Paul and some other prisoners were handed over to a centurian named Julius, who belonged to the Imperial Regiment. The next day we landed at Sidon; and Julius, in kindness to Paul, allowed him to go to his friends so they might provide for his needs... "Men, I can see that our voyage is going to be disastrous and bring great loss to ship and cargo, and to our own lives also." But the centurion, instead of listening to what Paul said, followed the advice of the pilot and of the owner of the ship. Acts 27:1b, 3, 10-11

Finding Good

Have you ever known people who did things you didn't like but helped you in some way or did nice things for you?

In my life there have been a lot of people that I didn't think were such great people, but had positive qualities despite their faults. I know people who are pushy, abusive, dominant personalities that will go out of their way to do good things for people.

Maybe you have people like that in your life... Maybe you have friends who boss you around or use you to get things or to places... But they might volunteer to help at church events, or help out in some other way when there's work to get done.

Look for the good qualities

I grew up hearing, "Well... You have to look for the good qualities." Which means stop complaining about how that person acts and remember that they do some pretty good things.

In Acts, Paul bumps in to a guy like this. He let Paul go see his friends. Pretty nice thing to do! But later Paul tells him they're heading for a storm and everything will get damaged and Julius chooses not to listen. So, Julius, even though he didn't do the right thing there, he did do something nice for Paul.

When you have people like this, you'll just have to take my moms advice to "look for the good" in those people and make the best of the time you spend with them.

Day 71

 Though while he lived he counted himself blessed -- and men praise you when you prosper -- he will join the generation of his fathers, who will never see the light of life.
Psalm 49:18-19

Power, Fame, Death

I'm always interested in learning about what people do to make sure they're remembered. I've read about people leaving lots of money to have their name placed on buildings, highways or stadiums. Those people worked hard to accumulate all this money, and just like everyone else... They died.

Of course, I don't know anything about these people... They may have been amazing people who left money to these organizations for the right reasons... But I bet some of them did it so they could be remembered after they die. Maybe in life they were powerful in business, respected by everyone.

I think people get so caught up with life on earth that it's all they think about. They worry about whether people will remember them and remember how many great things they did and all the worldly accomplishments that they achieved.

Life on earth is temporary

Today I picked a couple verses from Psalm 49... The last section of chapter 49 talks about people who had big houses, lots of riches and all the things that go along with having lots of money... But the last verse says, "A man who has riches without understanding is like the beasts that perish"...

In other words... If you're so caught up in life on earth and getting lots of money and things that you forget all things are gifts from God, life on earth is going to be the best thing that happens to you... Because you'll miss out on eternal life in heaven.

I'm not telling you to stop striving to be the best at whatever you choose to do, or to stop saving money or enjoy the things that money can buy... I'm telling you to always remember that your talents, which make earning money and having a good life possible, are given by God and you should always give credit for your success to Him...

Day 72

> Let me understand the teaching of your precepts; then I will meditate on your wonders. Psalm 119:27

Walk, Don't Run

You know what? I've been a Christian a long time. Know what else? I know a lot of people who are Christians... Some have been for a very long time, some are brand new, some in the middle. And... There are some things, beside the obvious, that we all have in common...

We all believe in Jesus. We all believe that he died for our sins... But remember, I said besides the obvious. A lot of the Christians I know, myself included... Don't really study the Bible regularly. A lot of us have never read the whole Bible, and if we have, we didn't really take the time to think about it and figure out how we can put it in our lives now.

In this book, we take passages and think about what the Bible is saying... But it takes you maybe 5 minutes to read and think about them... When I say study the Bible, I mean... Read a section (not just a verse) and really think about what it says to you. And not too many people I know do that.

Don't just read it... Apply it

The verse from today's Psalm tells us to read, understand and meditate on God's word. In James, we're told, "Do not merely listen to the word...Do what it says" (James 1:22). Now this is really a two-part thing... Read and understand it, then put it in action.

I think there are a few reasons why we don't study the Bible as much as we could... Believe it or not, time is not the issue. I think we try to run before we walk... We don't know where to start, get confused, overwhelmed and discouraged... It's not easy!

So, make an effort to study the Bible more. There are lots of great resources, Bible study groups and websites. Find something that you like (or start your own!) and commit to studying the Bible today.

Day 73

 "Therefore everyone who hears these words of mine and puts them into practice is like a wise man who built his house on the rock... But everyone who hears these words of mine and does not put them into practice is like a foolish man who built his house on the sand." Matthew 7:24,26

Weak Walls

Not too long ago I helped a friend do some construction work. I'll be honest with... I'm not very handy, I can't pound a nail in straight, nothing is ever straight... In the end... It's usually worse then when I started.

We looked like professionals. Old clothes, tools... Everything needed to build a border around a new pathway. We dug out the area, made it flat, mixed the cement, and started putting the bricks in one by one.

After 2 hours of work, we needed a break... We looked at the border... It wasn't even close to level. The bricks were all different heights. So... We took them all apart and started over, using a level to guide us... As we fit the last brick in place, I looked back just in time to see the first bricks falling apart and tipping over...

It's not even raining!

Maybe you're familiar with the story from our verses in Matthew for today. The rest of the story is, the person who built his house on rock still had his house when bad weather came... The house on sand crumbled in the bad weather... Kinda like the border I was building today.

While the border crumbled, I thought about how easy it is to question God when stuff goes bad. The storms from Matthew could be like bad stuff in our lives today. If your faith is strong, bad stuff doesn't knock you down, but if you don't practice what Jesus is teaching, you might question your faith and maybe even turn away from God!

I sometimes question why stuff happens... Maybe you do too... It doesn't make us bad people, it makes us human... But just remember that God has a plan for your life, and that even if your "walls are a little shaky" when bad stuff happens, if your faith is strong, and you really practice what Jesus taught, they won't fall over.

Day 74

> Therefore, I urge you, brothers, in view of God's mercy; to offer your bodies as living sacrifices, holy and pleasing to God -- this is your spiritual act of worship. Do not conform any longer to the pattern of this world, but be transformed by the renewing of your mind. Then you will be able to test and approve what God's will is -- his good, pleasing and perfect will. Romans 12:1-2

What's For Dinner

If you asked my mom, she might tell you that when I was a kid, how hungry I was depended on what she was cooking for dinner. If she was making something I liked, I was really hungry... If she was making vegetables or something else that I didn't like, I wasn't really very hungry at all.

If I asked my parents if for $5... The response was always, "Why do you want $5?"... It even happened with my friends sometimes... "Hey, you wanna do somethin?" with, "What you wanna do?" as the response.

These aren't trick questions, are they? They're very direct questions with pretty simple answers... But the answers weren't specific. Why do you think that is? Why can't people just answer questions? They know what is really being asked and yet they avoid a direct answer.

It all depends

I have a theory about these answers... The answer to all these questions (and lots of others) is dependant on the end result. If I ask a question and the answer to that question is another question... Like, "What are you going to spend the $5 on?" ... and my answer isn't acceptable, I probably don't get the money. It's conditional.

These are all simple examples, but how often do we do this with God? In Romans, we're told that we can know what the perfect will of God is for your life, but we must present ourselves to God and not be conformed to this world.

The point is, we usually want to know God's will before we decide whether or not we'll go along with it. God may tell you something that you don't want to hear. The question is, are you going to do what He says? If you want to know the will of God, you must present yourself to Him then accept His will, no matter what.

Day 75

Do you not know that in a race all the runners run, but only one gets the prize? Run in such a way as to get the prize. Everyone who competes in the games goes into strict training. They do it to get a crown that will not last; but we do it to get a crown that will last forever.
1 Corinthians 9:24-25

In Training

In a surprising turn of events, I ended up on the adults team and the kids won the Kids vs. Adults softball game. The old people couldn't throw, couldn't catch, and if by some miracle we got a hit, we were out of breath after running to first base. It wasn't pretty.

The kids had all kinds of energy. They were getting hits, were good in the field and ran the bases like they could have kept running for hours. They out played, out ran out pitched and won the game in the bottom of the 9th inning, when all of the adults were gasping for air.

The kids are more active, play more, have more practice... They're in better shape! Old people spend their days sitting behind desks and eating too much. The kids had the advantage of training that the adults haven't had for a L-O-N-G time.

Spiritual training

Even though the adults had to cook burgers for the winners, the victory was one that faded quickly. Like what Paul is talking about in 1 Corinthians. He's saying everyone works hard to win prizes and awards... Trophies and ribbons are great, but don't help in the long run.

We should train as hard for the spiritual battles of spreading God's word as we do for races and softball games. Most people who exercise can do push-ups, sit-ups, and other kinds of physical exercises... But how many people do spiritual exercising?

Concentrate on spiritual exercises. Prepare for the contests that matter forever! To help you, I came up with a spiritual fitness plan: Read your Bible and think about what God says. Spend time in prayer every day. Pray for others who need special help. Do a least one loving thing for someone each day. Try to please God in everything you do. Follow this plan and you'll be on your way to spiritual fitness.

Day 76

 The Lord is my shepherd, I shall not be in want. Psalm 23:1

Life On A Leash

Old Paramus Reformed Church sometimes has a "Blessing of the pets" service. There are all different types of pets... People bring their pets for treats and a special blessing from Reverend Marsden... He prays for years of happiness and love for all the pets and their families. It's great! And my dog, Maggie has to sit in the car and watch.

Maggie loves people and other animals... Too much. She gets excited and jumps up and barks and her tail goes a million miles an hour. I know she wouldn't hurt anyone, but sometimes people are a little nervous around her, so I decided that she needed a muzzle, a thing to keep her mouth shut, so she couldn't get in any trouble.

The service was about to start, Maggie had her muzzle on, and didn't like it... Not only did she have to stay right by me because of the leash, she had this thing holding her mouth shut. She cried, and whimpered, and clawed... So she had to be in the car.

The Lord is our shepherd

Maggie wanted to play. To have fun, run around, eat treats... Be a dog! But I know what's best for her. In this case, she either needed to be on a leash with a muzzle, or she couldn't be involved in the service.

There are lots of places in the Bible where you can find shepherds. Shepherds are responsible for watching, protecting and caring for their flock. In Psalm 23:1 David says, "The Lord is my shepherd" ... We're like his flock. We look to Him to protect us, provide for us and look after us because we're really helpless.

We have to realize that things are done for our own good. Just because I think it's safer for Maggie to be on a leash when we're out of the house doesn't mean she likes it, but it's for her own safety... Remember that you can't have everything you want, and sometimes it seems like things aren't fair... Maybe like you're living your life on a leash... But the Lord is your shepherd, and he knows what's best for you.

Day 77

> I have labored and toiled and have often gone without sleep; I have known hunger and thirst and have often gone without food; I have been cold and naked. Besides everything else, I face daily the pressure of my concern for all the churches.
> 2 Corinthians 11:27-28

A Day Off

Sometimes things get pretty stressful. It's been said, "That which doesn't kill you makes you stronger." Have you ever heard that? Now that I'm an "adult" I hear it a lot... I bet you do too.

People told me, "Just wait till you get older... Then stress really kicks in." But I see what young people go through, and I don't think stress is something that comes with age. Sports events... Music stuff, drama stuff, work... The list goes on and on... And lets not forget friends and havin fun!

I personally stress over other stuff... Getting things done on time (which I never do), money, work, school, what's for dinner, where that piece of paper went... It seems like stress never ends for me, and I'm sure for you too... So... I have a solution...

Take a day off

Aren't I smart? Sometimes we just need to get away for a while... Don't answer the phone, don't really do any work... Sit and relax. Play games, read, whatever. Just take it easy...

You know, it's true, what they say... That which doesn't kill you makes you stronger... Take Paul for example... He went through all this stuff... And came out a stronger Christian because of it... He did great things even though he had all these stresses in his life.

Paul didn't have to rush around to games or any of the other things that we stress about... But he used the stress that God put in his life to make him stronger... Do you? What do you stress over? How do you deal with it? The next time you start to stress, take time to sit quietly and think about Gods love and the peace that comes from that... Then pray His power will help you turn stress into strength.

Day 78

> It was not by their sword that they won the land, nor did their arm bring them victory; it was your right hand, your arm, and the light of your face, for you loved them.
>
> Psalm 44:3

What Is Safety?

I was maybe 10. I was in an aluminum rowboat with my brother. The weather forecast called for rain. Lightning was flashing. Thunder was booming. The waves were pretty big. And we were a long way from home. Probably not the smartest thing I've ever done. Definitely not very safe. In fact, very dangerous.

Thinking back, the list of less than safe, not too smart things I did is much longer than the list of safe, smart things I did... I was always doing stuff I probably shouldn't be. I think we all do things that aren't smart or safe.

I bet if you think about it you could think of lots of dangerous situations that you've been in. For example... Maybe you were outside after dark, ran across the street without looking, lit fireworks near apartment buildings or houses, went swimming after eating, or did other stuff...

What safety isn't

Even though like me, you have someone who tells you to stay out of dangerous situations because they want you to be safe... Is safety the absence of danger or the presence of God? God looks out for us when we so stuff. It's not luck, it's God's grace that keeps us safe.

There are so many times where God protected His people. He helped them survive and win wars, kept them safe through the bad times as well as the good times. I think today's verse from Psalms is reminding us of that.

Even though God keeps us safe we really shouldn't swing bats with people standing close, jump off a pier in ice cold water, or any of the other things we do that might not be safe. But remember to praise God for keeping you safe... And good luck trying to convince your parent that "Safety isn't the absence of danger" when you're trying to do something that isn't safe... It didn't work for me, either.

Day 79

 I appeal to you, brothers, in the name of our Lord Jesus Christ, that all of you may agree with one another so that there may be no divisions among you and that you may be perfectly united in mind and thought. 1 Corinthians 1:10

Who's Right?

Some of my favorite bands broke up even though they were very popular. I happens all the time! Groups split up and nobody can figure out why... They were making lots of money, selling lots of CD's, on tour with sold out shows...

Why does this happen? They have money, fame, popularity, and all the great stuff that comes with it. What could make them decide to break up the band? If you've ever seen interviews with bands, they all say how great the life is, and the only thing that matters is that people hear the music.

Most of the times, these people who all share the same goals split because they can't agree on how to achieve their goals. Maybe one wants to play one style of music, and another member wants to stay with what has worked in the past. Even though they all want the same result, they can't agree on how to get there.

Division is bad

Reformers, Catholics, Baptists, Methodists... All these different denominations, all with similar ideas... Who's right? What are the differences? How are they similar? Can people who belong to different branches of the church talk? Go to the same social functions? Be seen together?

There used to be huge fights about this stuff. Can you believe it? Protestants didn't talk to Catholics... I remember having friends who were Catholic. They thought they were right, I thought I was right... So we didn't talk about it... We just played baseball.

Paul writes that we should try to put aside our differences and remember that even though we disagree about things, we all believe that Jesus is our Savior; the only way to heaven is through Him; that we need to spread the word of God and do His work. Keep your eye on the ball. Remember what's important, and don't let division stop the work of God.

Day 80

> By the grace God has given me, I laid a foundation as an expert builder, and someone else is building on it. But each one should be careful how he builds. 1 Corinthians 3:10

Caution: Builders At Work

Sometimes the OPRCYouth! website goes under heavy construction. I spend days building the home page, making buttons, checking code, lining things up, making changes here and there. Usually after a few days I look at my progress and think to myself, "Wow... It's perfect. Everything looks just the way I drew it on paper."

When I'm building a website, I take the first page and use it as a template so all I need to do is change the text and all the pages look the same without me having to completely re-write every page. The first page takes days or sometimes weeks to build, but the other 200 pages can get done in a day or two.

One time I completed most of the pages and decided to take down the old site and put up the new one... Then I went to test it. The first page had errors on it... The buttons didn't go link to the right page, the title page had a spelling error in it... And, since that was the template... All 200+ pages had the same mistakes in them.

Be careful building

As I always do, I tried to take this "lesson" and figure out what I was supposed to learn from it. So I flipped to today's verse in Corinthians. Paul had a lesson for the people in Corinth, and it seems like he was talking to us today too...

He told the people in Corinth that he had built a strong Christian foundation in the community, and it was up to them to continue teaching others. But he was afraid everyone would teach the wrong information. One person teach something that wasn't exactly right and that lesson would get passed on to other people, and suddenly there would be a huge group of believers who had errors in their religion.

Paul wasn't trying to tell people to stop, he was reminding them keep learning and studying so they could teach others. Today we need to help other people understand Christianity and God's love for us, but we also need to be careful so we spread God's word truthfully and accurate.

Day 81

{ Therefore encourage one another and build each other up, just as in fact you are doing. 1 Thessalonians 5:11 }

Little Rays Of Sun

As you go through life, you might wonder if you're doing a good job, appreciated by others, making a difference, admired, looked up to, needed, respected, loved... You'll go through times where everything will roll along and you'll feel good about what you do, and you'll have times where you really wonder if what you do is worthwhile... When it's good, it's amazing... When it's bad it's really depressing.

There will be days when it seems there is nothing good that can possibly happen. If you're lucky, you'll have someone in your life... young or old, who will send you a card, an e-mail, a note, pick up the phone or drop in with a bit of encouragement.

I get lots of encouraging messages. I get e-mail from all over the world, notes from kids in church, praise from my pastor, cards from my mom and kisses from the dog. And you know something? These are the most important messages anyone can send me. I save them all so when I'm having a bad day, I can read through them and know that someone cared enough to write.

A little encouragement

I remember reading a quote from someone famous... Mark Twain, I think... He said, "I can live two months on one good compliment." People all around you need a little encouragement once in a while. So we should always be looking for opportunities to praise people... Sincerely.

In today's verse Paul reminds us how important affirmations and compliments are. In Ephesians he tells us to build others up according to their needs (Ephesians 4:29). I call these little pick-me-ups 'little rays of sunshine' because both make me feel a lot better when I'm having a bad day.

Think about who you know that may need a little ray of sunshine... It doesn't have to be a lot... You don't even have to spend any money! Knowing someone took the time to care makes people feel better.

Day 82

 The eyes of the arrogant man will be humbled and the pride of men brought low; the Lord alone will be exalted in that day. The Lord Almighty has a day in store for all the proud and lofty, for all that is exalted (and they will be humbled).
Isaiah 2:11-12

Look What I Have

Lots of great stuff is happening at OPRCYouth! Our events have been noticed by the newspapers, and have been picked as "Top 10" events by a major youth worker magazine, kids have been coming, learning about Jesus, becoming Christians... And I had almost nothing to do with any of it.

Have you ever wanted the whole world to know about something? Maybe you got a new toy, a new car, all A's on a report card, new bike, some award for something... You went around to all your friends and family and told them all about it... Only to find that they seemed excited, but you could tell they were a little jealous or not interested...

Maybe in your excitement you said something like, "This is so great! I got all A's on my report card!" Most people, myself included, are always excited about their own stuff... Completely normal, by the way... But most of us, in telling others about this great thing keep using "I" ... "I did this", "I got that"... We're bragging.

Glorify God... Not yourself

I get jealous when people are talking about their new houses or cars. Right now, I don't have those things. I try to be excited for them, but sometimes I get tired of listening to people brag about their stuff or their success...

Isaiah is reminding the people of Judah (and us) that bragging is bad. He says, "The eyes of the arrogant man will be humbled"... Think for a minute... Do you think bragging takes glory away from God?

The next time you start telling someone about something that happened, or something you got, remember how you feel when people brag. I know it's hard when you have something good you want to share but remember to give the glory to God... Think for a moment about how you might do that the next time you get ready to tell someone all about your good news.

Day 83

 For whoever would love life and see good days must keep his tongue from evil and his lips from deceitful speech. He must turn from evil and do good; he must seek peace and pursue it. 1 Peter 3:10-11

Gotcha!

I remember it like it was yesterday. April 1. I got up in the middle of the night, walked quietly down the steps from my bedroom to the kitchen. Took a rubber band out of my pocket and wrapped it around the button on the "sprayer hose" that was part of the faucet. I also remember the shriek when my mom turned the handle on expecting water to come through the faucet and instead getting sprayed by the hose...

I love practical jokes. I was always playing pranks on people. I was part of a group of people who handed marbles to the principal at graduation, put bubble gum in a fellow students trumpet to see what would happen...

Have you ever had someone play a practical joke on you? Have you ever done it to someone else? Have you ever had them go bad? Maybe you did something trying to be funny and caused someone to have hurt feelings, or caused damage to something... At what point does a practical joke turn from fun to dangerous or hurtful?

Is intent an excuse?

I didn't mean to cause damage to that car when I stuffed a rag in the muffler... But I did. Is it possible to know whether a prank will be harmful or funny before you do it? What about losing trust when you play a joke on someone? These are sometimes the result of practical jokes...

Peter saying that we tell lies or do evil things... Is he talking about pranks? Maybe not, but he was talking about living without doing harm because that is the way to peace.

When someone plays a joke they may be in some way dishonest depending on the joke... Who's really being hurt by that dishonesty? The person who the joke was played on? The prankster? The point is that we have to really think about the results of a practical joke before we go forward with it...

Day 84

> "His eyes are on the ways of men; he sees their every step. There is no dark place, no deep shadow where evildoers can hide." Job 34:21-22

Big Brother

Have you ever seen the show Big Brother? The idea of the show is simple... Watch a bunch of people live in a house, see how they act and get along with other people. There are cameras everywhere.

The show title comes from people who thought (some still do!) the government was getting too involved in our lives. Convinced phone calls were being listened to, medical records looked at, bank accounts checked... So, someone started the phrase "Big brother is watching"...

"You better watch what you're doing... 'Big Brother' is watching..." I guess there are a couple arguments to be made here... Some people say, "We should be watched ... If we're not doing anything wrong, it doesn't matter who's watching..." Others say, "It's not their right to know what we're doing... If we break laws, they should find us without watching every step we take..."

The REAL 'Big Brother' is watching

Think about all the jokes about God or someone 'waiting at the pearly gates' with a book to determine who was allowed in heaven. Sure, they're just jokes... But in Job 34, we're told there's nowhere to run, nowhere to hide... God sees everything we do.

Knowing that God is watching my every move and knows all my thoughts makes me a little nervous. In every day there are things that I don't want God or anyone else to know about. That knowledge certainly makes my decision making process different.

God is all knowing... What's really amazing to me is... Even though He knows everything I say, do and think, all the good AND all the bad, He still loves me. I don't think of God knowing everything as a scary thing, but instead a source of comfort and extreme love for me. I hope you do too.

Day 85

 Then he said to Thomas, "Put your finger here; see my hands. Reach out your hand and put it into my side. Stop doubting and believe." Thomas said to him, "My Lord and my God!" hen Jesus told him, "Because you have seen me, you have believed; blessed are those who have not seen and yet have believed." John 20:27-29

The Earth Is Round?

Years ago, great thinkers believed the earth was flat and at some point boats would fall off. Not too long ago astronomers thought there weren't any planets other than the earth and sun. More recently, you probably wouldn't believe the Detroit Tigers won a World Series or that the New York Yankees had teams that were terrible.

All these things may seem random to you but there is a common theme to all of these examples. All these things can be proven. It can be proved that the earth is round, there are lots of planets, the Tigers actually won a World Series (sure, it was way back in 1984 but still...), and in the early 90's the Yankees had really bad teams.

In the case of the earth being flat, the great thinkers of the day had no way to prove that the earth was round. Same thing with the planets... Scientists had absolutely no way to prove that there were more planets in the solar system. These guesses were completely based on faith.

Faith is believing in something that can't be proved

Jesus challenged Thomas to feel the marks where he had been nailed to the cross because Thomas didn't believe that Jesus could be alive. Even though Thomas heard that Jesus had risen after being crucified, he just couldn't quite be convinced until he actually touched the wounds.

How much different are we? We don't always believe things until they're proven to us... Like when our parents tell us not to touch the hot stove because it will hurt... How many of us did it anyway? But when it comes to being Christians, we have faith that God exists, even though we can't see, hear or touch Him.

Even though we can't see God with our eyes we may sense his presence and "hear" his voice at times, but faith in God is believing in what cannot be proved.

Day 86

> How long will you lie there, you sluggard? When will you get up from your sleep? A little sleep, a little slumber, a little folding of the hands to rest -- and poverty will come on you like a bandit and scarcity like an armed man. Proverbs 6:9-11

Ants!

Sometimes I wish I could go back to a time where things were easier. Sleeping in, watching TV, playing sports... The good life. The funny thing is, I think my memory is a little altered, because now that I think about it, I started getting jobs when I was 12 because my mom and dad wanted me to understand the value of hard work (and pay for my own baseball cards)...

How many times have your parents told you not to sleep so much, or watch too much TV? How many times have they asked you to do chores or, (get real!) read a book? I mean seriously...

During the school year you probably spend around 30 hours in school, 5 hours doing homework, 20 hours on the Internet doing "research" (Hey, John! Did you see that tie Mr. Whoever was wearing today?), 10 hours playing and practicing for sports teams, 10 hours with friends, 10 hours watching tv... And that doesn't even include sleep! Doesn't anyone understand how busy you are? You need a break!

Wake up!

Our verses from Proverbs 6 talk about sleeping too much and being lazy and the problem with that... Earlier in the chapter we're told to be more like ants because they work hard... And it reminds me of the cartoon where the ants work hard preparing for the winter when food will be hard to find and the grasshoppers starve because they were too busy playing.

I know life is busy... All these things that you want to do... Sometimes you need a break from all the craziness... But that doesn't mean you get to sleep all day...

The writer of this Proverb is telling us to work hard like the ants do... Get up and help around the house... Mow the lawn, do some cleaning, help with the laundry... Or go out and get a part time job... The next time you need to be reminded about getting work done, think back to the story of the ants.

Day 87

> Shout for joy to the Lord, all the earth. Worship the Lord with gladness; come before him with joyful songs.
> Psalm 100:1-2

Finding Joy

I don't do much that isn't fun. Sure, there are chores that I have to do that aren't all that much fun, but there is even fun in those sometimes... If I do stuff with the youth group at church, you can bet it's going to be fun. Playing drums? Fun. Going to a game? Fun. Sounds pretty selfish of me, huh?

Come on though... Be honest... Most of the things you do are driven by emotion... You eat ice cream because it makes you happy. You play because, hello! It's fun and makes you happy. Shopping? Happy. Television or video games? Fun. Swimming? Fun. Sleeping in? Happy. Collecting something? Fun.

And it works the other way too... Cleaning, taking out the garbage, homework, broken toys... All bad... They're all things we want to avoid as much as we can... Take a look at your day and just see how many of the things you do (or don't do) are driven by emotion.

Putting the JOY back in Christianity

Someone asked me a question the other day... If being a Christian has all these rules, how can it be any fun? At first, I wasn't sure how to respond. Being a Christian doesn't always mean we're going to have fun. But, as I was thinking about this, I started making a list of words that could describe fun... Guess what I found?

On my list were a couple words... Joy: an emotion of sudden pleasure. Rejoice: Feel joy and gladness. I went a little further to see how many times they are in the Bible. Depending on what translation you use, the word "joy" appears in around 170 verses in the Bible... Rejoice is in 145 verses.

There are verses that show people from the Bible being happy, verses that tell us to be joyful, times when we're told to praise God with great joy and happiness... And that's just the beginning! So the next time someone asks me how being a Christian can be fun, I'll have the answer, and I hope you will too.

Day 88

> Moses said to them, "It is the bread the Lord has given you to eat." Then Moses said to them, "No one is to keep any of it until morning." However, some of them paid no attention to Moses; they kept part of it until morning, but it was full of maggots and began to smell. So Moses was angry with them.
> Exodus 16:15b, 19-20

Pack Rat

Sometimes start the biggest project ever. It takes days, sometimes weeks! I ache, get cuts on my hands, argue with myself, laugh and cry... Sounds pretty dramatic, right? I go through all the stuff I've accumulated throw out what I don't need anymore because my room is a mess.

It's true... I admit it. I'm a pack rat. In my office, around my computer is books, papers, notes, drum sheet music, computer cables, CD's... And lots of other stuff... And even though I hate to admit it, most of this stuff will never be looked at... Ever.

I know lots of people that have this problem. Maybe you're not one of them, but I bet you know someone who does. Maybe there's a closet full of clothes, toys, shoes, baseball cards, pictures...

Be daring!

Exodus tells us about people who have been holding on to stuff for thousands of years. Now, the reason the Israelites were holding on to the manna isn't the point for today... But, the fact is, they were holding on to stuff, just like some of us do today.

Holding on to stuff might be a symptom of something more serious. Maybe we're afraid to try new things! We want to hold on to what worked before because... It worked before... Why try anything new? Maybe we're afraid to find new ways to worship, tell people about Jesus' love for us, or invite new people to church or to youth group events.

We can learn from the Israelites. They were told to throw out the manna after one day! It was to encourage them to be bold because what they did worked before! Take this lesson to heart... Be bold! Find new ways to get new energy, insights and knowledge instead of relying on the same old way of doing things...

Day 89

 During the fourth watch of the night Jesus went out to them, walking on the lake. When the disciples saw him walking on the lake, they were terrified. "It's a ghost," they said, and cried out in fear. Matthew 14:25-26

I Believe In Miracles

Have you ever heard the miracle defense? "I didn't do that! God put my finger prints on that door even though I wasn't there!" I bet you'll never hear the "miracle defense"... People would laugh the accused right out of the courtroom... "God put your finger prints there... Yeah... Right... How stupid do you think we are?"

Most people don't believe in miracles these days, but yet, I hear the word used a lot... "I got an A on my test! It's a miracle!" or, "It's a miracle I got to school on time" or, "I found my shoe under all the clothes on the floor... It's a miracle!" Those aren't really miracles. They can be explained. I got an "A" because I studied, got to school on time because I didn't have breakfast... You get the idea...

But miracles can happen

What is the definition of **real** miracles and why don't people believe they can happen? My Webster's dictionary says, "A miracle is the act attributed to a supernatural power." Something that can't be explained. Maybe we're too smart to believe in miracles.

In the Bible there were miracles. Things that couldn't be explained... There is no way to explain how Jesus was able to walk on water, or any other miracles in the Bible. If walking on water isn't a miracle, I don't know what is. And Jesus' disciples were scared and thought it was a ghost! They were scared because they couldn't find a reasonable explanation for why Jesus was able to walk on water.

Today, people don't believe in miracles because everything has to be proven by science. And if it can't be proved by that method, either it didn't happen, or there has to be another explanation for it. We're "too smart" to believe that God could make things happen when science says it isn't possible... But that doesn't mean it's true... I believe in miracles, and I hope you're "smart enough" to believe in them too... God is all-powerful and works beyond what science says is possible.

Day 90

 "Be careful not to do your 'acts of righteousness' before men, to be seen by them. If you do, you will have no reward from your Father in heaven." Matthew 6:1

The Right Reasons

Sometimes I work at a homeless shelter. Sometimes I cook, help everyone get settled in, and some stay over night to make sure everyone gets up for work in the morning. I always think it would be a good idea to help out, so I sign up to help.

Would my "good deed" be as good if I did it so kids at church would see me doing it and take part? If I did it so people could see good I am? If I worked so people would say "thanks" to me?

Have you ever done volunteer work? Why? Did you get the response you thought you would? It's only natural to want some kind of "thank you" for taking time out of our day to help someone else out... What's the difference between expecting a "thank you" and hoping that everyone notices you were working?

Be a servant

Matthew tells us to do things for the right reasons... "So when you give to the needy, do not announce it with trumpets," (6:2). Then we'll be rewarded by God. Not people seeing what we do and thanking us, or seeing how hard we work and follow our lead, or any of the other reasons that we may try to do "good deeds" and volunteer work.

Read Philippians 2:1-11. In this passage we're told to follow Jesus' example. He walked the earth a servant, just like a regular guy. He walked, talked and taught people even though he was the Son of God. He was so humble, even as he was sentenced to die on a cross... And for that, he was exalted to the highest place and given the name above every name...

So today, think about ways you can help someone this week. What kind of expectations do you think you'll have? How can you be happy and content no matter what response you get from the people you're helping? Be a servant today... Find a way to follow Jesus' example.

Day 91

> Commit your way to the Lord; trust in him and he will do this: He will make your righteousness shine like the dawn, the justice of your cause like the noonday sun. Psalm 37:5-6

Calendar

I usually try to fill in my calendar months in advance. All the meetings and events for the youth groups at Old Paramus, class schedules, weddings, dates I have to speak at conventions... You may be wondering why I write down things that are going to happen in 3 months?

Commitment. If things are written down, I'm sure to do them... If I wait until the last minute I won't want to have a meeting, and it's easier to change or cancel if it isn't written down...

Have you ever said to your parents, "Sure, I'll help you," only to find out that on the day you were supposed to help your parents, something fun was happening? Are you going offer to help next time? Or will you try to put off making a decision until you find out what else is happening on that day...

Make a commitment!

Sometimes we're like this with God, too... We commit to Him and say we're going to change the way we live, but when something more fun comes along, we forget about that promise to God and go have fun anyway... What kind of commitment is that?

When you back out of things with your friends and family they probably forget about it... Unless you do it all the time. Then they might stop asking you to do stuff, or keep reminding you that you agreed to do something. Fortunately Gods isn't like that. He's always waiting for us to make a true commitment to Him and not worry about what we'll be asked to do or what we'll have to give up to keep our promise.

Making a commitment to God is a scary thing, but Psalm 37, says, "Delight yourself in the Lord and he will give you the desires of your heart." If we commit ourselves to the Lord and trust in him, "He will make your righteousness shine like the dawn." Remember the promise in Psalm 37 and decide to renew your commitment to God today.

Day 92

{ In the beginning God. Genesis 1:1a }

Alphabet Soup

Well, today something amazing happened. I was eating soup (that's amazing in itself!) and as I dipped my spoon in to the bowl, I glanced at how the letters in my alphabet soup were arranged. As I read the words that were formed in my bowl of soup, I realized the letters and words were a devotional!

Have you ever thought about how the earth was formed? How life began? Maybe you studied the "Big Bang" theory or thought about evolution... These theories say life just started on it's own... A chemical reaction took place and, poof! A living cell.

The little bit I remember from high school science is that cells have all these parts that have to line up just right or they don't become cells. Do you think these things could just line up right without any help? That would be like me opening a can of soup and finding today's devotional spelled out in my bowl...

God created the heavens and the earth

All the ideas about how life started are impossible. Even scientists who try to prove these theories are frustrated because they've run out of new ideas and all the old ones are wrong. In fact, here's a quote from a scientist... "More than 30 years of experimentation ... has led to a better idea of the immensity of the problem rather than the solution." (Klaus Dose, Interdisciplinary Science Reviews 13, 1988)

Some famous scientist said something like, "if we received a single message from space, we would know there is intelligent life." But scientists still can't prove how life started. The only reasonable explanation is that God created life... That is the message we keep getting... So why do we have to keep trying to prove differently?

In the beginning God created the heavens and the earth... He made something completely new... He created the universe and everything in it. Take time today to read Genesis 1, and remind yourself of all the things God created... but remember that important phrase, "In the beginning God."

Day 93

Unless the Lord builds the house, its builders labor in vain. Unless the Lord watches over the city, the watchmen stand guard in vain. Psalm 127:1

When I Grow Up

Race car driver, astronaut, fire fighter, fighter pilot, baseball player, rock drummer, movie star, sports announcer, millionaire, successful businessman, motorcycle builder, professional golfer, teacher, motivational speaker, best employee... Now, you might be wondering what this list is all about.

At some point in my life, it was my dream to do each of these things. Some of these dreams lasted a long time (some I still have!) and some lasted only hours... But I wanted to be everything on that list.

I was pretty lucky to have people around me who supported my dreams, even though they were sometimes unrealistic. My mom and dad knew that I was never going to be a professional golfer, but they bought me golf clubs anyway. When it was my dream to be a musician, they supported me by getting me lessons and buying me instruments.

Dream a great dream...

I bet you've daydreamed about being or doing something. Have you ever tried to make a list of all the things you dream about? What do you want to accomplish? What do you want to be

I think Psalm 127 is talking about dreams. Just like the builders and guards our dreams aren't possible without God... This doesn't mean that God will grant us all our dreams... I'm STILL not a professional drummer or baseball player... Because those dreams were selfish, not necessarily what God had in mind for me.

I think we all need to remember who's really in control. We can achieve dreams, through hard work and dedication, but our dreams are really dependant on God. Make sure that when you're chasing your dreams, you remember to look at achieving your dreams through God's eyes and not your own... God may have a different vision of success than you do.

Day 94

> "'Rise in the presence of the aged, show respect for the elderly and revere your God. I am the Lord.'" Leviticus 19:32

You Know You're Old When

Every Wednesday, I spend time with a group of older women who get together to make quilts. We were eating cake, laugh, tell stories, and live life the way it was meant to be lived...

It always amazes me how wise these women are. They've seen everything, experienced a lot of things and have lots of good advice to give... I just can't figure out why the world seems to forget and ignore older people... Maybe we're too busy doing other things and just don't have enough time for these wise people.

How many elderly people do you know? Grandparents, older neighbors, people at church... I bet you know a lot! I try to spend time with the older people in church because I think they are amazing Christians. Their faith is so strong and I always hope some of that faith and wisdom will find it's way to me!

You have all the answers, but nobody asks you the questions

I wish I had enough time and space to share with you all the "old people" jokes I know... But jokes aside, I always feel extra special when I'm around older people. They make me laugh, make me cookies, make me think, make me feel important and make me remember that I don't know everything.

We're told to show respect to the elderly... Why does God care whether we do that? Because we can learn so much from them? Avoid making mistakes they've already made? Maybe we're told to spend time with the elderly because it will benefit both us and them! They feel special, loved and admired... Can you think of some way spending time with older people might benefit you socially or spiritually?

I hope that you spend some time finding ways to spend more time with the older people in your family, neighborhood and church... It will be time well spent for you and them.

Day 95

 Be patient, then, brothers, until the Lord's coming. See how the farmer waits for the land to yield its valuable crop and how patient he is for the autumn and spring rains. You too, be patient and stand firm because the Lord's coming is near.
James 5:7-8

A Microwave World

The other day I was warming up food for lunch. It was the longest 2 minutes of my life! I was hungry, the TV show I wanted to watch was starting, I was in a hurry! That ham and cheese sandwich was taking forever to heat up and I was getting more and more frustrated by the second...

I'm impatient. And I'm not alone. I think the whole world is sometimes. We want everything right now! Food, information, news, someone to love, new toys, new cars... Whatever it is, we can't get it fast enough. Everything you use every day was invented because someone was impatient.

Waiting is hard to do

Have you ever been so impatient that you couldn't wait another second and ate something that wasn't done cooking? One of God's favorite lessons is patience. Think of times in the Bible where people had to be patient... Moses, Job, David, Paul, the Israelites... The complete list is almost as long as the things we have because we're impatient!

We get impatient waiting for God to reveal his plan to us, or to let us know what we're supposed to do, or show us why we have to suffer, or for Jesus to return... We want everything now! But God doesn't work that way, and because of that, patience is a lesson we often have to learn over and over.

What are things you've been waiting for God to answer in your life? What is he trying to teach you through patience? Think about how you can strengthen your patience... Maybe through prayer, by focusing on something else, or maybe by forcing yourself to wait for something you really want... Whatever it is, remember not to fall in to the "Microwave mentality" of always needing things right now.

Day 96

> But the man who looks intently into the perfect law that gives freedom, and continues to do this, not forgetting what he has heard, but doing it -- he will be blessed in what he does. James 1:25

Torn

I keep busy. School, work, church, helping people, playing drums, sports, cooking, going out with friends... I'm always torn by "the right thing to do" vs. "what I'd really like to do"... I always try to "do the right thing" but it's sometimes a struggle.

Pretty much everything I do is driven by "doing the right thing"... Helping people out, studying the Bible, spending (or not spending) money on stuff, taking classes and studying hard for them... The point is, I always try to do the right thing... Do you?

I'm sure there have been times where you knew what "the right thing to do" was, but didn't do it... Maybe you knew you should help out with a project at church, but avoided the phone call (or returning the call) of the person asking for your help. You really didn't feel like doing the right thing.

Giving in to the right thing

The "right thing" doesn't always mean helping out with things, it could also be treating people with respect or a lot of other things... Sometimes I wonder why nobody is doing "the right thing"... Thinking of my own life, I think there have been times that I didn't do what was "right" because I thought it was much more difficult than doing what I wanted... In other words, I was selfish.

The chapters from James talk about "doing the right thing" and the rewards for it. Take time to read and think about verses 22-27. It's clear that people who don't "live the word" are fooling themselves. Verse 27 tells us that the true service of God exists in charity towards our neighbors, especially those who need the help of others.

God made us with a natural sense of what's right. Spend some time today thinking about some of the actions Christians should take... Are you doing those things? Focus on ways that you can really change from just hearing God's word to living it. Pray that God will help you find the strength to do what's right in your daily activities, going out of your way to honor Christ.

Day 97

> Though he stumbles, he will not fall, for the Lord upholds him with his hand. Psalm 37:24

Kicked In The Teeth

Some days are pretty rough for me. There are some days I get up, not quite sure why I've been placed in the position I have... Those days are usually following bad experiences or criticism from people. Or when something didn't go the way I planned it... Which is only about everything I try...

Sometimes it's silly things... A bad lesson or when nobody shows up to a youth group event. Sometimes it's criticism from a parent, meant to help me, but taken by me as a negative, and it makes me question my ability to do the job I was called to do.

Have you ever had that? Maybe you were criticized by a coach, teammate, parent or teacher. Maybe you were trying to tell someone about Jesus and didn't have such good luck. It's hard to bounce back from those experiences. I call it "getting kicked in the teeth".

Don't give up!

We have such high expectations for something and it flops or doesn't work out quite like we wanted... And it seems the whole world notices it. It's very hard to bounce back from that... Especially if you're human... And we all are!

Today's verse from Psalm 37 is talking to us though... Even when we stumble in our lives, we won't fall because God is right there with us. In our lives there are going to be days where we wonder why we're setting ourselves up to "get kicked in the teeth", but we can take comfort in the fact that God won't let us fall.

The fancy word for "getting back in the game" is perseverance. "To persist in something started"... So, we're called to do God's work, and we know that sometimes it's going to be hard. We're going to make mistakes, we're going to get criticized for our work or just plain rejected, but we have to press on and continue, no matter how hard it is... God's work isn't easy, but the rewards are amazing... Remember today's verse from Psalm 37 and pray that God helps you persevere through the tough days.

Day 98

> Brothers, if someone is caught in a sin, you who are spiritual should restore him gently. But watch yourself, or you also may be tempted. Galatians 6:1

Crutches

In the last few years, one of my sisters has broken an ankle... Twice! The breaks were pretty bad, she had a cast on her foot and couldn't walk for quite a while... When she did start walking, first she needed crutches then a cane.

Have you ever had an injury that required you to use crutches to get around? I think it's kind of embarrassing because everyone sees that you're hurt and tries to help you. What happened? How're you feeling? And all you want is to get back to your normal life...

Fortunately, for most of us, the extra support is only necessary for a short time, and hopefully we make a full recovery, get back to our regular lives and don't ever have to use those crutches again.

Christian crutches

If crutches are used for support because of an injury, what kind of support is there when someone you know is having a bad time with their relationship with God? Maybe they have an addiction to something, stealing, cheating... Whatever the situation... Where can they go? Who can they talk to? Where are their crutches?

Read Galatians 6:1-5. The whole section talks to us about our responsibility to help other people without pointing the finger of blame toward them. The verses also tell us to not get dragged down by other people's situations... We need to be "Christian crutches" to our friends and family and stay strong in our faith and keep temptation under control...

Everyone has a burden to carry at one time or another. As a member of the body of Christ, we must keep our eyes open for brothers or sisters struggling under a weight and help them get through their situation. How can you help someone carry a burden and not get dragged down by that situation? It's hard, but we're called to be "Christian crutches" ... Praying for the strength to help someone with a burden.

Day 99

> Repent, then, and turn to God, so that your sins may be wiped out, that times of refreshing may come from the Lord.
> Acts 3:19

Please Insert Coin

One of my favorite things to do is play video games. I go to an arcade, figure out what game I can play the longest for $5, and buy tokens. I figure I can play a while and have a good time until my money is spent.

The characters in the game shoot at me, throw things, hide behind things and sneak around while I try to get them all and move through the first level. I get jumpy, breath heavy, my pulse races, and then it happens.

The words, "Please Insert Another Coin To Continue" appears on the screen. I put more coins in and continue. About 2 minutes later, those dreaded words flash again... More coins, more excitement...

It works in video games... But...

Don't you wish the idea of simply "inserting more coins" worked in other areas of life? I bet there are a lot of times in your life that inserting more coins to continue would come in handy... Is "forgiveness of sins" one of em? It is for me... I wish I could put in another coin and just go on without having to do anything to receive forgiveness...

Unfortunately, it doesn't work like that. All through the Old and New Testament, forgiveness is promised. I bet there are 20 places in the Bible that says our sins will be forgiven... But it's not as easy as putting more money in a machine and continuing with life... There are conditions... In Acts, we're told that we have to repent, believe that we will be forgiven, and confess our sins. In Psalms, we're told to pray that even though our sins are great (we sin a lot), they will be forgiven.

We're going to mess up sometimes. Maybe a lot, maybe once in a while. But, we're all going to. Thankfully we have a forgiving God who is willing to forgive our sins, if we follow the conditions in the Bible... Even though He doesn't have to... God is good! When you pray today, make sure to remember to thank God for being such a loving, forgiving Father.

Day 100

{ Finally, be strong in the Lord and in his mighty power.
Ephesians 6:10 }

Bad Boys, Bad Boys...

I was cruising along, minding my own business. The radio was blaring, I was tappin my feet and singing... Driving along on a beautiful summer day... I looked in my rear-view mirror and saw red and blue flashing lights swirling around and around... I quickly went through a mental list of the things I may have done, but couldn't think of any...

Maybe you've seen people being pulled over by police officers... How often is there just one police car? Almost never. They never know what they'll find, so there are usually two or more cars of officers as back up. Well, my situation was no different. As I sat there, first one, then two other police cars pulled up... "Boy," I thought... "With all these police cars, anyone looking must think I robbed a bank or something..."

I didn't rob a bank, in case you were wondering... I was speeding... And all these officers came to make sure everyone was safe. They could find really dangerous people in the car, and officers know it. They have a respect (not that they think bad guys are good, but they're aware of the danger) for people who might be dangerous.

...Whatcha gonna do

Just like officers respect danger, we need to respect the danger of Satan. We're not strong enough on our own to win a battle against him. We need to be aware of his strengths, weaknesses and abilities... Satan is not only dangerous, he's powerful!

We're told to, "Be strong in the Lord and his mighty power" because Satan really wants to separate us from God. He wants to get between us... As soon as he does that, we're easy targets... Satan knows we're too weak on our own, and the only way he can win the battle is to get between God and us.

The only way we can really beat Satan is with the power of Jesus. He's our backup in the battle with a dangerous opponent. So, "Be strong in the Lord" stay close to him and don't let anything get between you and God.

Day 101

> Open my eyes that I may see wonderful things in your law. I am a stranger on earth; do not hide your commands from me.
> Psalm 119:18-19

Ready To Assemble

I spent at least an hour putting together something that should have been done in 15 minutes... About half the time was wasted trying to get the pieces to line up and connecting them... The other half was wasted trying to figure out the instructions!

Have you ever tried to read instruction books? Even the English version looks like a foreign language... Pictures that show what goes where, short descriptions that don't make sense, ten different possibilities, but none exactly like yours...

This is why projects take twice as long as they should... It would be faster if I didn't read the instructions at all... Do you read the instructions before playing a video game? Plug it in and figure it out as you go... Right? But that's frustrating too... It would be so much easier if instructions were clearer...

Speak English, man!

Who writes these instruction books? They must understand what the instructions say... Why they don't look at it like the people who are buying the product? That's why I think the Bible is so amazing... It's our instruction book for life... And it's written so that we can figure it out!

Today's verses remind us that the answer to questions and problems can be found in the Bible... There are a lot of verses that tell us this... 2 Timothy 3:16-17, for example. The Bible was written long ago but the people who wrote it were given the words by God... And we can still understand it today!

The next time you're faced with a question or a problem, don't skip the instruction book... I know sometimes it's hard to find the answers in the Bible, which is why I suggest you get a book called a concordance... It helps you find the topic in today's language and find the verses that will help you. Don't forget to praise God for giving us "Life's Instruction Book" in a language we can all understand.

Day 102

> Stand firm then, with the belt of truth buckled around your waist, with the breastplate of righteousness in place, and with your feet fitted with the readiness that comes from the gospel of peace. Ephesians 6:14-15

Cleats

When I was young and played little league baseball, I wanted shoes with spikes on them... Cleats. I thought having those shoes would make me run faster, hit better, catch more and help my team win more games.

Now, I realize that all those things I thought would improve didn't have anything to do with wearing cleats, but at the time, I thought it was important. Have you ever played sports? You probably wanted or needed cleats too... But I'm sure you know that shoes won't make you run faster, kick harder or any of the other silly things I thought would be improved by wearing them.

The real reason athletes need cleats is to gain traction and protect their feet. Hitting a foul ball off your foot wearing cleats still hurts... But not nearly as much as if you were wearing regular shoes. And you may not be able to run faster, but you won't fall as often with the added traction.

Shoes as armor?

In Ephesians, Paul is talking about spiritual armor, and comparing it to "regular battle armor". Some things he mentions I can understand... But shoes? A shield is important because it protects from the advances of the enemy... Same thing with a breastplate...

So... What's with the shoes? Our feet are pretty vulnerable to injury. If I was fighting a war, and had all this armor to protect me, but stepped on a nail or sharp stick, I wouldn't be able to keep fighting! Just like in real war our feet are vulnerable, in a spiritual attack, we have weaknesses too...

So, shoes are an important part of this story... Shoes have traction and help keep us from slipping as well as provide protection for us... When we're fighting a spiritual war, it's important to keep our footing and not slip and fall in our faith, and to protect our weak areas.

Day 103

 The one who calls you is faithful and he will do it.
1 Thessalonians 5:24

Obstacle Course

One of the kids from church went to football camp. He'd been pulled, pushed, twisted and stretched... And that was before the real workouts began. Then he was chased, tackled, piled on, and bruised. Every day he thought there was no way he was going to get through camp and make the team.

Sometimes I make obstacle courses. With things to crawl under, step over, weave through, and poles to climb. While balancing a cup of water on a hat. Kids look nervous, thinking there is no way to get through the course without getting soaked.

Olympic athletes train their whole lives to compete for two weeks. The swimmers are in the pool all day; gymnasts stretch and work on routines; runners do exercises to build muscle, cardiovascular exercises, stretching... A lot of athletes talk about the struggle of staying focused. Most of them say they considered quitting lots of times!

Life is an obstacle course

Harry made the football team, all the kids made it through the obstacle course, and the Olympic athletes got to perform. They all worried about making it through the hard times... They all probably considered quitting... But they realized that after all the struggles, they could look back and see that the overall experience was good, even if it didn't seem so while they were in the middle of the bad stuff.

Life is one big obstacle course. Sometimes we can't see the benefit until after we struggled. When that happens, we look back and say, "Wow! I made it!" We can look back and see how God allowed us to get through those times, and the spiritual growth we experienced as a result of those obstacles.

When I sit back and think about all the obstacles I've overcome in my life, I feel better because I realize that even when it didn't seem like God was in control... He was! When you're in the middle of a difficult time and it seems almost impossible to continue, Remember God is providing grace to help you through the obstacle course...

Day 104

 For where two or three come together in my name, there am I with them. Matthew 18:20

Crowd Control

Sometimes it's frustrating to be in a group and have only one other person there. I get enthusiastic about all the groups, and I look forward to studying and having fun. But it's hard to keep that enthusiasm when the group is two people.

I think a lot of people share this frustration. A lot of young people have Christian websites, start study groups, or lead worship services... And they get frustrated because they feel like they're doing God's work, and can't figure out why nobody is coming! They get frustrated and stop doing these things.

Sometimes I plan things and get frustrated or sad if only a few kids show up... Sometimes I even change my lesson completely if there aren't "enough" kids that come. I try to stay positive and present the lesson I feel God told me to teach, no matter how many people are there... But it's hard!

Hear and obey

The world tells us the number of people who show up determines success. Concerts have been cancelled because of slow ticket sales... Church services have been changed or cancelled because there weren't enough people coming...

If we're following what we feel God is telling us to do, it shouldn't matter how many people come. Some of the best teaching sessions happened when only one person came... God placed in my heart that I needed to teach a specific lesson, and by His grace, the people who really needed to hear that message came. Now **THAT'S** success.

Being led by God often means we shouldn't use the world's standard for success as our measuring stick. You never know what an act of obedience will yield at the time. We must leave results to God. Our role is to hear and obey. His role is to bring results from our obedience. Ask God to give you a willingness and ability to hear the Holy Spirit and to obey His calling.

Day 105

{ Behold, I am coming soon! Revelation 22:12 }

Ready?

Not until: I graduate high school... Live on my own, get married, have kids, have enough money, own a house, graduate college, find a career I love, travel all over the world, am successful, earn respect, get a hole in one, bowl a perfect game, learn how to play the drums better than anyone else, stop sinning... Not until tomorrow...

Even though people pray for Jesus' return, there are conditions like the ones above. We want Jesus to return, but not until we do all these things. Maybe we're afraid we might really do something sinful and aren't ready to put all our sinful ways behind us... Maybe its just selfishness.

Maybe you have these same thoughts. Maybe you're so busy thinking about all the stuff you have and want to do that you haven't even given a second thought to when Jesus might return... You've probably sung songs that ask for Jesus' second coming, but still you have that list of things you really want to do before that day comes.

So... Are you ready?

Revelation 22 reminds us to be ready today. We need to be better Christians... We can't pray for Jesus to return... Then silently hope that we get our "to-do list" done before that happens. We need to be ready today!

Read Revelation 22... It's amazing! The book of Revelation speaks of some pretty terrible things, but chapter 22 is really uplifting. Whoever is thirsty, let him come. We're thrown a life preserver! In verse 14, "Blessed are those who wash their robes, that they may have the right to the tree of life and may go through the gates into the city." And in verse 17, "Let him take the free gift of the water of life."

Pray for the second coming of Jesus... Make sure you're ready. No more conditions... Continue doing what you're called to do... Live a holy life, bring others to know the love of Jesus, and stop making excuses for why tomorrow would be better than today... Because Jesus says, "Behold, I am coming soon!" Amen. Come, Lord Jesus.

Day 106

> Jesus replied, "Love the Lord with all your heart and with all your soul and with all your mind. This is the first and greatest commandment. And the second is like it: Love your neighbor as yourself." Matthew 22:37-39

Back To Basics

Sometimes when I practice the drums I practice rudiments. Rudiments are basic stick patterns. I do them because I get so caught up in learning new beats and songs that I forget to really improve my technique to become a better player.

In the fall the first few days of school are always the same. Review material from the last year, because the stuff you learned last year was important for the new stuff you'll learn this year.

If you play sports, I bet the first few days of tryouts or practice the coaches have you practice skills you haven't practiced for a long time. If you play softball or baseball, you practice throwing the ball at the chest of your partner, or fielding ground balls. If football, hockey or lacrosse is your sport, maybe you walk through basic plays because those are the fundamentals of the game.

Fundamentals

Sometimes we need to "go back to basics"... Practice and do things that are fundamental skills and habits for some activity that is usually really easy for us. So it only makes sense that we should do the same with our Christianity.

The Great Commandment from Matthew 22 sums up the 10 commandments in two sentences. The first 4 commandments, Have no gods before me, have no idols, don't misuse God's name and keep the Sabbath holy fit under "Love God with all your heart, mind and soul". The remaining 6, Honor parents, do not murder, no adultery, no stealing, no lying or coveting all boil down to "loving your neighbor as yourself".

Sometimes we need to go back to basics and remember that in our daily lives the 10 commandments fall under two statements from Jesus. Sometimes I think it's easier to remember to live those two statements than try to remember all 10 commandments. Focus on living by God's law, no matter which method is easier for you.

Day 107

{ Each of us should please his neighbor for his good, to build him up. Romans 15:2 }

Random Acts Of Kindness

At some point in your life you've done something kind for someone. It may have been something really big, or something small. Maybe you mowed someone's lawn, baby-sat, picked something up for an older person... Or something else... without expecting to be paid or getting something in return.

I'm always amazed at the acts of kindness that I benefit from. People are always willing to help me with things and everyone who volunteers says they're happy to give a little bit of time... "No big deal, Joel!" But I appreciate their acts of kindness even if it is something small.

I've seen lots of people helping others. Older people do things to help young people and the other way around! I've seen people help others by giving money, time and talents. I've been on both ends of acts of kindness and I bet you have too.

It may not be the act itself

In most cases, it isn't the act itself, but the thoughtfulness and sacrifice of DOING it. For example, your parents saying, "Wow... It was so nice of you to think of taking out the trash without being told!" -- That you thought of taking out the trash was just as important as actually doing it.

Our verse today from Romans is only one example where we're commanded to be kind to others... There are other places too... Right in Genesis there are examples of "random acts of kindness"... Like when the Hittites tell Abraham that he can have his choice of tombs to bury Sarah, in verse 22...

Look for opportunities to do "random acts of kindness" for people. Keeping in mind that these acts don't have to be huge things, it's the thought that counts... Take the time to help someone out. The Bible tells us how important kindness is... So take the time to show kindness in some way every day.

Day 108

> The heavens declare the glory of God; the skies proclaim the work of his hands. Psalm 19:1

A Light Bulb Moment

Have you ever had someone explain something to you? A teacher, friend, parent, or purple dinosaur? Have you ever been just as confused after an explanation as before?

Pretty frustrating, huh? There have been so many times that I've been in this situation. I sit back and think, "Gee, Joel... You must be really clueless if you don't get it... Everyone else seems to understand..." Sometimes, it's because I'm concentrating... Other times no matter how hard I concentrate, I just don't get it.

Then it happens. A moment of clarity. Suddenly, after the 10th time of having that algebra formula, scientific theory or Bible story explained it all becomes clear. Everything falls in to place and what stumped us or kept us a little confused seems like the most obvious thing in the world... It's a "Light Bulb Moment"...

Your own "Light Bulb Moment"

I've read the Bible so many times I couldn't even begin to count. I memorize Bible verses, and the Bible has been a major part of my life. But even I have light bulb moments. Something I've read hundreds of times jumps off the page and I can't believe I missed it all those other times!

While reading Psalm 19, I glanced up over the page of the Bible at my computer wallpaper. It's a beautiful picture of the sun rising... The colors are brilliant! And I thought, "Wow! The heavens DO declare the glory of God..." Those gorgeous colors were created for us! All the colors in nature that we take for granted every day were created for us to recognize and praise God for his handiwork.

Reading the Bible is so exciting because every time we read it, we see something new! Every time I read it I have a light bulb moment, and I bet if you read it with an open mind you will too. Praise God for letting us understand His written word and have "light bulb moments".

Day 109

 Since my youth, O God, you have taught me, and to this day I declare your marvelous deeds. Psalm 71:17

Good Habits

Have you ever seen the movie Mrs. Doubtfire? In it, the after-school nanny, Mrs. Doubtfire takes care of three children. On the first day, she makes the kids turn off the TV and do their homework before dinner. The oldest child makes a comment and Mrs. Doubtfire makes them clean the house, then sends them to do their homework.

Maybe you've read about bad habits and how they get in the way of worship. But you know, not all habits are bad. I remember my parents encouraging me to develop good habits... Studying, praying before dinner and bedtime, reading instead of watching TV, going to church, tithing...

Just think about all the good routines and habits you have, all because of your parents? Brushing your teeth, eating vegetables, getting enough rest, exercising, doing volunteer work, I bet you can think of a lot more than I have...

...Stay with you

There are a couple ways to look at being young... This is your chance to mess up and do things you'll regret later in your life, or your chance to set a positive pattern for your life. As you go through life, you'll probably (I hope!) continue taking showers every morning, brushing your teeth every day and doing all the things that have become or are becoming habits for you now.

The person who wrote Psalm 71 was really praising God for helping him develop good habits when he was young. He was encouraged to praise God and have hope in safety and salvation as a child and those things have stayed with him as an adult! He praises God over and over for those habits.

Some habits will stay a part of your life forever. Maybe you're fortunate enough to have people in your life to encourage you to develop good habits and continue doing Gods work... Let those good habits become part of your life right now, no matter how old you are, and continue to follow them each and every day.

Day 110

> So the word of God spread. The number of disciples in Jerusalem increased rapidly, and a large number of priests became obedient to the faith. Acts 6:7

Brave New World

Not long ago you could only find "Christian" television shows on late at night and on stations nobody ever watched. If you wanted to listen to "Christian" music on the radio you had few options: old (and I mean OLD!) hymns and church services...

It was hard to even BUY up-beat contemporary Christian music. Christian books? Only in Christian book stores... Hang with other Christians? Sure... But not the popular kids... And only at church... And you definitely didn't invite your friends to church or youth group because it wasn't cool.

A lot of people who were Christians a few years ago didn't brag about it. They didn't tell anyone. They tried to fit in to the regular world because they didn't want to be known as "those people"... "Those people" cornered non-believers on the street and wouldn't let them leave until they took a flier... Stood on street corners with signs, or stood in front of stores trying to get attention. and tell people about their religion...

Times have changed!

It's a brave new world. In only a few years time, we can watch Christian television in Prime Time on major networks! If you flip through the stations on the radio, you're likely to hear great Christian music that'll make you tap your toe and praise God! Huge bookstores are adding Christian books to their shelves.

We're told to spread the Gospel. And it's cool to do that again! You don't have to be shy about asking your friends to go to youth group or church... It's a whole new world, filled with people who are just WAITING to be invited to a Christian event.

Take advantage of this change in the world... You can do lots of things to encourage your friends, family and neighbors to learn more about Jesus. You don't have to be "preachy" with them... You can invite them to fun things where they'll be exposed to a Christian group and message... Take advantage of this brave new world today.

Day 111

> In him we have redemption through his blood, the forgiveness of sins, in accordance with the riches of God's grace.
> Ephesians 1:7

Face Only A Mother Could Love

How many times in a day do you get disapproving looks from your parents? Think about it for a minute. Maybe you forgot to do your chores, didn't do homework, ran over minutes on your cell phone... I bet in a day or two you do a lot of things that might not be what your parents would approve of.

It seems like I'm always making mistakes. If I'm not doing something wrong, I'm probably sleeping... And even THEN I may be doing something wrong. How about all the things we THINK of that are wrong? If I counted those things I'd really be in trouble!

When I was younger, I remember hearing people joke about "You're so ugly you have a face only your mother could love!"... No matter how ugly a kid is, parents always think their kid is beautiful. When we do things our parents don't approve of, they eventually forgive us, even when nobody else would...

Another nail

The Sermon on the Mount in Matthew is pretty scary! Jesus is giving us all these rules that we have to follow. And it's hard to do that... In Matthew 5:19 Jesus says, "Anyone who breaks one of the least of these commandments and teaches others to do the same will be called least in the kingdom of heaven."

Who can possibly live up to the standards in the Sermon? Nobody can... We're all going to break these rules. There are going to be when we're going to be mad, think impure thoughts about someone we see... But you know what? God is our parent too... Even when we mess up, he forgives us...

I saw a video of a retreat where everyone had a nail and walked up to a cross and pounded it in. God sent Jesus to the world, and he was killed on a cross... For us... As Christians we believe that. We believe Jesus died to save us from our sins... Every day we experience the grace of God when our sins are forgiven.

Day 112

{ Jesus wept. John 11:35 }

What If God Was One Of Us?

Lately there has been a lot of people hearing bad news. Powerful storms tearing apart homes and families, the constant fighting in Iraq and other places in the world, families hearing about the loss of loved ones. I bet they're going through a lot of emotions. Shock, anger, sadness...

These are extreme situations that I hope you never have to experience. Aren't we all sad about things sometimes? Sometimes I wonder how God can let bad things happen. Doesn't God understand we're emotional? Doesn't he know how bad we feel when something terrible happens to us? "Come on, God!!" we scream... "Enough is enough!"

Sometimes I think animals have it easy. They don't have the same emotions. Animals don't cry at night because something bad happened. God created people who experience emotions... He must not have been thinking clearly, because if he really understood emotions, wouldn't he have wanted us to be spared the bad ones?

God WAS one of us

I keep getting that song stuck in my head... "What if God was one of us? Just a slob like one of us..." What makes us human is emotions, God was one of us... He had to deal with all the emotions too... Happiness, sadness, anger... Wow! God really DOES understand what we're going through...

All through the Bible there are examples of our God showing emotions... There were times where we were told he could be angry like in Psalm 7, times Jesus was sad and wept... God and Jesus did have the whole range of emotions... So when we go through them, we can't really say God doesn't understand what we're experiencing.

Praise God today for giving us emotions... Praise God today for being our creator and understanding what we go through, in good times and bad... It's great to think that God knows exactly how we're feeling because he's experienced emotions even more strong than what we feel... Thank you, God, for walking a mile in our shoes.

Day 113

 The word of the Lord came to me: "Son of man, you are living among a rebellious people. They have eyes to see but do not see and ears to hear but do not hear, for they are a rebellious people." Ezekiel 12:1-2

In One Ear, Out The Other

You need to change your diet! Too many carbs, not enough vegetables, too much candy, WAY too much pizza... No more ice cream... Did I mention eat more vegetables? Your cholesterol is too high, you're too heavy... Blah, Blah, Blah...

People are always giving advice. Don't sit so close to the TV... Don't read in the dark... Your radio is on too loud... Wear your seatbelt... Don't go swimming right after you eat...

All this advice is given with Christian love, I'm sure... They want us to be healthy and safe... But if you're like me, you don't always listen. The advice goes in one ear and out the other... Sound familiar?

Are you listening to me?

Do you think the people who give you advice get frustrated when you don't listen? It must be so hard to love someone so much and have them completely ignore you. Have you ever tried to tell your friends they need to change their ways and start a relationship with God? Have some of them ignored you?

Ezekiel had it rough... He kept trying to tell people to change their ways. Did they listen? NO. He kept saying, "the word of the Lord came to me", hoping the people would realize he was speaking on behalf of God... But it didn't work. They probably knew he was right, but didn't want to give up their sinful ways.

Ezekiel didn't give up though. The people needed to hear the message, even if they didn't listen. Just like your parents are doing their job when they tell you to turn down the radio so... Just like you do when you tell people about how God has made a difference in your life. Your words may go in one ear and out the other... You can't control that, but make sure you don't stop telling people, even when you get frustrated that they aren't listening. The Holy Spirit will work in those people's hearts when it's time... They're hearing you, even if they aren't listening right now...

Day 114

 Come to me all you who are weary and burdened, and I will give you rest. Take my yoke upon you and learn from me, for I am gentle and humble in heart, and you will find rest for your souls. For my yoke is easy and my burden is light.
Matthew 11:28-30

Stressful Times

Doesn't it seem like we have way too much stuff going on? School, homework, practice for sports, part-time jobs, helping out with chores at home, spending time with friends, youth group activities, community service projects...

The list of things we have to do is endless! It seems like we'll never get it all done... Sometimes we don't! It's hard to concentrate on getting things done (or sleep!) when we're overloaded and stressed out about all the things we need to do.

The list of things that need to get done keeps growing, and everything needs to get done or we feel like we're letting people down... That's a lot of pressure! We get so stressed out that don't even have extra minutes.

25 hours in a day

Yep... We all have the same thing. We all have too much stuff that we absolutely need to get done... I figured out how to get more hours in a day... Stay up later and get up earlier. The problem is, if you're like me, you get all stressed out and the first thing that gets cut off the "to-do" list is time with God.

I think Jesus is talking about the burden on our souls from sin and the rest that comes from forgiveness of those sins. But believe me, this can also apply to physical stresses and burdens. By coming to Jesus every day our souls are stronger and that allows us to focus on what's important and makes dealing with the stress of overload easier.

Jesus is calling us to "Take his yoke" and become disciples. Followers. By following his example and spending time strengthening our relationship with him he is sharing our burdens and making the weight of all those things that cause us stress a little less. Find rest today (and everyday!) with Jesus. Find a few minutes every day to share your burdens.

Day 115

 To the Lord your God belong the heavens, even the highest heavens, the earth and everything in it. Deuteronomy 10:14

Total Control

It was a dark and stormy night... Not really... It was dark, but the sky was as clear as crystal. The moon was shining brightly and the stars were twinkling beautifully. What I'm describing to you is the skyline in New Jersey one night.

I live near a major airport and noticed extra twinkling lights in the sky. Of course, they were airplanes. That's not so unusual (although it is unusual to be able to see them so clearly), what struck me was the number of planes that were up there, and how organized they were.

A person was sitting in a tower at Newark Airport watching a screen and making sure the planes were all where they needed to be, in the proper order, at the right altitude... And it changes every 30 seconds because the planes are landing and new ones are coming in and going... These people must be really busy! They have all this responsibility to make sure everyone is safe.

If God is your co-pilot...

You're in the wrong seat... I saw this on a bumper sticker one time. Pretty cute, huh? Just think though, these air traffic controllers are controlling only a small space around their airports. Imagine a God so powerful that he controls everything all over the world! Every little thing that you can imagine is at your God's control.

I'll be honest with you... That is so incredible to me. When it rains, snows, when the skies are clear or cloudy... Every situation we're in every day... Who we meet, what we do... Everything is controlled by God.

I wonder if maybe you think, "That whole 'If God is your co-pilot' thing has no place in this message... You might be right... But think about what that is really saying... I'm sure you've seen the "God is my co-pilot" stickers... But this is different... If God is in control of everything, he's really the pilot... Don't you think? Thank God today for being in control.

Day 116

> The Lord is slow to anger, abounding in love and forgiving sin and rebellion. Yet he does not leave the guilty unpunished; he punishes the children for the sin of the fathers to the third and fourth generation. Numbers 14:18

Two Sides

A number of years ago, people could buy anything from Sears and Roebuck. Whether they wanted clothing, swimming pools, toys, or tools, Sears and Roebuck had it. As time went along, the store sold still everything, but Sears was known for its tools.

The brand name "Craftsman" was what people thought when they heard Sears. They had every tool in every size imaginable... Anyone who used tools, mechanics, dads, professionals... Used tools from Sears... And kept em in a "Craftsman" tool box.

In the late 80's (yes, I'm old!) even though Sears still had everything, all people bought was tools. Everyone was so focused on "Craftsman" tools that they forgot Sears sold other stuff. So Sears started advertising "The Softer Side" ... Reminding people that Sears sold more than just tools.

The other side of God

Sometimes I think Christians need to see ads that focus on "The other side of God". I know different denominations stress different things... Some stress the happy, forgiving side of God, some focus on the God who sends people to hell. I'm not one is right or wrong... But sometimes we need to remember that God has two sides.

In my church, we always hear "Slow to anger and abounding in love" -- The "softer side" of God... But we rarely hear the rest of that verse, "Yet he does not leave the guilty unpunished." In Numbers, God punished the people by making them live in the wilderness for 40 years until all the adults who wouldn't obey had died. Often we stop reading before we get to that part of the story.

My hope is that every now and then you stop to consider the "other side of God" -- No matter what your church stresses, the loving God or the punishing God... Take some time to remember that God is an amazing God... We have the best of both worlds! A God who loves us... But who also punishes us when we mess up.

Day 117

 We have different gifts, according to the grace given us. If a man's gift is prophesying, let him use it in proportion to his faith. If it is serving, let him serve; if it is teaching, let him teach; if it is encouraging, let him encourage; if it is contributing to the needs of others, let him give generously; if it is leadership, let him govern diligently; if it is showing mercy, let him do it cheerfully. Romans 12:6-8

All Wrapped Up

Try to remember all the gifts you got for Christmas three years ago. I bet you can't remember them all, and I bet if you can, you haven't looked at or used those gifts in a very long time.

I know that's the case with my own gifts. Over the years I've been given books, toys, musical instruments... You name it, I've probably received it as a gift. All those things were used for a while, then tossed aside for something newer, better, faster (louder!)... They were all things I wanted, but have since stopped using.

If you think about it, I bet you could make a huge list of things you were given and don't use, even though you begged someone to give them to you. You just HAD to have that toy. Eventually your parents or someone else gave you those gifts.

Spiritual gifts

Maybe you're thinking, "What are spiritual gifts?" Well, let me tell you... Spiritual gifts are extraordinary gifts of the Spirit given to Christians to help them do God's work. Some of them are mentioned in today's verse from Romans, but there are a whole bunch of them...

Spiritual gifts change, too. I've had different gifts that were given to me to use. You'll have the same thing. God will give you a specific gift so you can do something special, and those things will probably change!

Today we're thinking about all the gifts we've forgotten about or don't use. What a shame it would be for us to receive these amazing gifts from God and not put them to use. We're given these gifts, all wrapped up, tied with a beautiful bow... All so that we can do the job God has called us to do...

Day 118

> So the women hurried away from the tomb, afraid yet filled with joy, and ran to tell his disciples. Suddenly Jesus met them. "Greetings," he said. They came to him, clasped his feet and worshiped him. Matthew 28:8-9

Soothing Voices

When I get a cold my voice sounds really raspy under the best of circumstances... And at the worst, it's little more than a whisper. Why do I tell you this?

Not to get sympathy or candy. But because when I don't have a voice, I think about all the emotions that can be brought out by voices. Think about it for a second... So many of our conversations have different messages based on the tone of voice.

Parents may use the same words when they're really mad, but you know if they're joking by their tone. Or the tone your parents use when you're upset... You know, that soothing, soft voice. See my point? Tone of voice makes all the difference.

The soothing voice of Jesus

The voice I love the most is when a person is trying to make me feel comfortable or better when I'm feeling sad. The voice filled with love and kindness. Soft and tender that just makes you think, "Wow... I feel so secure." Parents are pro's at this voice. They always know how to use their voices to make us feel better.

Just imagine how excited and scared Mary Magdalene and the other Mary must have been when this angel came down and spoke to them. They must have been so sad that Jesus had died and now they're seeing this angel! I know how scared I would be in that situation. But then Jesus met them and with one word soothed them. I'd like to think that his voice was soft and gentle...

His voice must have been really something at that moment because these two women, as scared as they were fell down and worshiped. Even today I sometimes imagine the soothing voice of Jesus. If I'm having a bad day, freaked out about something or just need some support... I imagine Jesus speaking to me in that soft voice and suddenly I feel much better. I hope the next time you need a soothing voice to make you feel better you're able to hear the most soothing voice of all... The voice of Jesus telling you everything will be ok.

Day 119

 God did this so that men would seek him and perhaps reach out for him and find him, though he is not far from each one of us. Acts 17:27

Rule Of Three

Health = Diet, exercise, rest. School = Listening, participating, studying. United States Government = Legislative, Judicial, Executive. Plant growth = Good soil, water, sun. Maggie's (my dog's) life = Eat, sleep, play.

All these things fit in to my rule of three. When I think of these things I think "balance". All the things I mentioned above are balanced. We often hear that word when we think of health too. We're told that to be at our best we need to pay attention to more than one part of our life.

If spend all your time, playing video games, you'd be out of shape from not exercising. You would probably fall behind in learning because... Hello! No time for school... How about if you spent all your time studying. You'd be really smart, but you wouldn't have any friends. Dates? No time for that... Your life would be out of balance!

Is your relationship with God balanced?

As Christians we need to work on our relationship with God. Sure, we spend time worshipping God at church. We pray when we need or want something. Try to do the right thing. But are we really having a relationship with God?

Having a balanced relationship with God and developing a friendship with him takes more than just those things "when we have time"... I think a relationship with God is another "Rule of Three". Relationship with God = Prayer, Bible study, worship. We need to pray. And not just when we want someone to be healed or we forgot to study for a test. When I say Bible study, I mean spending time figuring out it fits into your life. And worship means more than going to church.

I've been thinking about this particular rule of three (of course I've forgotten about that whole "health" rule of three, but that's another story). If it seems like you've been stuck in your relationship and haven't been growing, I'd urge you to try following this rule of three and put your most important relationship back in balance.

Day 120

> When they had gone, an angel of the Lord appeared to Joseph in a dream. "Get up," he said, "take the child and his mother and escape to Egypt. Stay there until I tell you, for Herod is going to search for the child to kill him."
> Matthew 2:13

Sweet Dreams

My favorite memories from when I was a child are of my mom saying, "Good night, sweet dreams!" My eyes would close, and I would drift off to sleep with those words swirling through my mind... Some nights were filled with "sweet dreams" some with nightmares... I still have dreams (and nightmares, too!) ... Do you?

I have very clear memories of being chased, hurt, scared, lost and all alone. But I can't remember any of the "sweet dreams"... In fact, I almost never remember good dreams... Even the ones from last night! I remember being in the middle of a great dream... But I can't think of any of the details.

How often does this happen to you? You're in the middle of the perfect dream... You're all comfortable. Then it happens... The alarm starts buzzing, you hear people making noise, a car door slams or the dog cries at your door (Go away, Maggie! It's the WEEKEND!)... And you're awake. You might try to think about that good dream, but it's gone. Fuzzy. You can't quite figure out what was happening.

Run, man... Run!

But those nightmares... No problem remembering those, right? For some reason, those dreams stick with you. Maybe you get up and can't get back to sleep, you get a "midnight snack", turn the light on, check for monsters in the closet...

So just think about this dream that Joseph had. He must have been the happiest man on earth. His wife just had a baby... He was a dad! He's sleeping soundly and an angel pops into his dream... If that isn't weird enough, it tells him that King Herod is trying to find and kill his son. Now that's a dream you wouldn't forget.

So even all those years ago people remembered bad dreams... If that had been a "sweet dream" he might have forgotten it and history would be much different! So, even though the last thing you'd probably think to praise God for is a bad dream... Remember that this bad dream was a very good way to send an important message.

Day 121

 "If your brother sins against you, go and show him his fault, just between the two of you. If he listens to you, you have won your brother over." Matthew 18:15

Nice Doesn't Cut It

Listening to politicians is frustrating. Hearing candidates bash each other over who did or didn't do what. I'm tired of hearing them point out the others flaws. But you know something? We can take a lesson from them.

Have you ever had a friend who you knew was doing something wrong? Stealing money or taking illegal drugs? Maybe (I hope!) nothing that serious... But you knew and had to decide whether to say something and risk losing a friend or not say anything...

Your friend is making a mistake, doing something wrong -- what do you do? The world today tells us not to say anything that might be upsetting. We've become so afraid of hurting someone's feelings that we have stopped trying to correct bad behavior... It's easier and less stressful to be nice.

Tell it like it is

Sometimes we need to worry less about being nice and really get back to being able to tell people when they make mistakes. If you knew that someone would tell a teacher or another adult that you cheated on a test, wouldn't you be less likely to do it?

If you know someone is doing something wrong, you should say something about it. Now, you might be thinking about the verse that talks about watching out for yourself before pointing out flaws in other people. There needs to be a balance... We are responsible for our own actions and flaws, but shouldn't we speak to others about their mistakes?

Maybe this is part of what the world is missing? If people knew they would be confronted when they did something wrong, would they try harder not to do those things? Don't forget... It goes both ways. You'd hear about it when you mess up, too.

Day 122

> My son, pay attention to what I say; listen closely to my words. Proverbs 4:20

I Know You So Well

There are people you know very well, right? A best friend, parent, teacher, youth pastor, boy or girlfriend, coach... You know this person so well you sometimes complete their sentences. You know what they're thinking, how they'll react in certain situations... You know everything about them.

How often do you hear the first part of a conversation and the end of the conversation, but the middle part is filled with "blah blah blah..." You can tune out what they're saying... You already know how the discussion is going to go. You focus on something else, like what you'll say back, or how unfair this situation is...

Lets use money as an example. You're talking to your parents about getting a raise in your allowance... Again. You explain why you need more money. They come back with the usual, "You don't need more money because... " At about that point you start thinking, "How can I convince them that I need more money?"

Are you really listening?

If you're thinking of something else, how can you be listening? In order to make a good argument for more money, shouldn't you concentrate on what they're saying? If you really spent time listening, would you have a better chance of getting that bigger allowance? Probably.

We do this with God, too. We know all the rules. We know what the Bible says. We know God so well that while he's sending us clear messages and instructions, we're busy thinking about how unfair God is being to us... We don't really listen!

Today I want to encourage you to listen. Really listen. Don't think you know what your parents, God, and everyone else you think you know so well is going to say. If you're having a conversation, don't let your mind wander. Really listen. The people we know here on earth, and your heavenly Father all deserve to have your full attention.

Day 123

> And this is love: that we walk in obedience to his commands. As you have heard from the beginning, his command is that you walk in love. 2 John 6

Just Show It

We all have people we love. Parents, a boy/girlfriend, brothers or sisters, friends, grandparents... Hopefully we tell those people often that we love them. Everyone likes to hear that they're loved. But... Do you show those people that you love them?

You know what I mean... Show your parents that you love them by helping out around the house or being extra kind. Send your friends and family a note or e-mail. Just to let those people know you love them. Those kinds of actions mean so much to people!

One of my favorite songs is from a band you've probably never heard of... Extreme. It says something like, "if you showed me you loved me, you wouldn't have to tell me because I'd already know." (I could sing it for you, but it would hurt your ears!) When I hear it I think to myself, "Self... You don't really show people that you love them..."

Just do it

We could do little things to show people how much we love them... But we don't. And what about God? I'm always telling God how much I love him... I try to show him, by my actions... Sometimes it works, sometimes it doesn't. Sometimes I completely forget that it's not enough to just SAY, "God, I love you." Maybe you forget sometimes, too.

It's important to show God you love him... We can show God how much we love him by obeying his commands. Sure, it's easier said than done... We can't buy God flowers, volunteer to do the dishes or take out the trash... But we can listen to and obey his commands.

Show someone how much you love them... Do something extra thoughtful today... Buy some flowers, clean up the house, or help with dinner... Do something to show your love... And show God how much you love him, too. Obey the commands he's given and focus on showing your love instead of just saying, "I love you."

Day 124

> Does the rain have a father? Who fathers the drops of dew?
> Job 38:28

Post It Notes

Ah, yes. The little sticky notes. Possibly the greatest invention in recent history. Just enough glue to stick to stuff, but not so much that you can't pull them off. Write on em, stick em to the wall, and (in theory) remember important things. "To Do" lists, phone numbers, messages, times of appointments.

In my house there are post-it notes everywhere. I need post-it notes to remind me what the original post-it note was. They're everywhere! If you haven't figured out how great these things are, you will soon... They come in all shapes, sizes and colors and somehow, even with these great little sheets of paper... I forget stuff.

Sometimes on rainy days people complain... No matter what the weather, it seems there is someone who isn't happy... Too hot, too cold, too damp, too dry... It's always something. Nobody is every completely satisfied with the weather.

A reminder

Well, I have a post-it above my desk, right in front of me. It says, "God creates and controls everything." Sometimes I get so caught up in what's going on -- Rain, dry, cold, hot, cloudy, sunny -- and complain about it, that I need to be reminded of that simple fact... God creates and controls everything.

I was reading in the book of Job. Take some time to read chapters 38 and 39. These chapters really remind us about God's greatness. All the things he created and controls. It's pretty amazing if you stop to think about it. You'll be amazed at what you forget about.

Sometimes in our busy lives, we need a "Post-it" note to remind us of God's greatness and power. Sometimes my Post-it is rain. Maybe something else will remind you. But don't forget to stop and think about God's greatness, even in the small things like rain...

Day 125

> Then Moses raised his arm and struck the rock twice with his staff. Water gushed out, and the community and their livestock drank. Numbers 20:11

No Offense, But...

There is only one thing that is sure to follow "No offense, but..." -- Something offensive! No offense, but, that is the ugliest outfit I've ever seen. No offense, but, have you gained 50 pounds? No offense, but...

When was the last time you heard someone say, "No offense, but, that was an amazing play!" It doesn't work that way. Somehow, we think by saying, "no offense" it will be easier for the other person to hear. We don't want to hurt anyone's feelings when we're going to say something mean... Right? What are we thinking?

As soon as I hear those three words, "No offense, but" I get nervous because someone is trying to lessen the impact of what they're about to say. I've heard it a lot! That was boring. Have you gotten fatter? The other youth group I go to is much better. No way! I'm not flying down an icy hill on a piece of cardboard!

No offense, God, but...

I hate to admit it... I've said this to God a few times. No way, God... I'm not going to work for a church! Most people have probably at some point in their lives said, "No offense, God, but..." Maybe we don't have enough faith that the situation will work out... Whatever... But most of us have said it.

Moses said, "No offense, God" in the verse today. God told him everything would be ok, but he struck the rock with his walking stick anyway. Sure, water came out. But everything would have been OK even if he hadn't. Because God said so.

So I want to encourage you to take the words, "No offense, but" out of your vocabulary. Don't use them when talking to friends, parents or anyone else... And don't use them when you're talking to God. Even if it seems like God is leading you somewhere you don't want to go or putting you in uncomfortable situations, he knows best.

Day 126

> However, I consider my life worth nothing to me, if only I may finish the race and complete the task the Lord Jesus has given me -- the task of testifying to the gospel of God's grace. Acts 20:24

Why Bother?

Have you ever wondered why? Why you get out of bed, go to school, have friends, study, play sports, or go on dates? You do stuff... Why? Because you have nothing better to do? You're bored?

Maybe you watch TV to relax... Study to get good grades, get a good job, and buy a nice car... Eat because you're hungry... Everything you do is done for a reason. Make a list of all the things you do in a day and try to figure out why you do those things.

Every activity I do I try to think about why I'm doing it or what I want to happen because of that activity. In our youth group, there are some nights where the object of the night is for kids bring friends and have fun. It wouldn't be smart to make them memorize Bible verses or spend three hours praying with them.

Life on a wheel

We all need to start activities or projects with the end in sight. If you aren't sure why you're doing something, bad things could happen. Say you're writing a letter to a friend. You want to be friends, but you don't want to see them every day. You wouldn't write, "I don't ever want to see you again." You choose your words carefully.

Have you ever seen the little hamsters run on one of those wheels in their cage? They run and run. And they don't ever go anywhere! Sometimes I guess we all feel like that... But if you start thinking about being a Christian, you'll see that you should always start by thinking of the desired result: testify to the gospel of God's grace. Share your faith with people who aren't Christians.

If thinking about the end result is important when starting a project or activity, think about how important it is as you live your life! How would your life change if everything you do focuses on praising God and sharing his love with people who aren't Christians? Begin with the desired result in mind.

Day 127

 Shout aloud and sing for joy, people of Zion, for great is the Holy One of Israel among you. Isaiah 12:6

Sale!

Sometimes when I go shopping I drive in circles for 15 minutes to find a parking space, fight people in the aisles and through random piles of clothing. Then wait ten minutes for a fitting room, wait twenty minutes to pay, walk cautiously, dodging cars until finally, I get back to the car. Why is shopping so crazy? One word: SALE!

People are crazy! Shopping carts crashing, people running around trying to get the last item, pulling their friends or family this way and that to get to what they're looking for. People get crazy when there are sales.

The funny thing about sales is people can find sales on most days, but because a store advertises special savings stores are packed with excited, happy people.

Ho-Hum

When was the last time you got as excited about God as you did when a new game or those jeans you've wanted a really long time went on sale? You might be thinking, "Come on, Joel... You have to be kidding... We're talking about something I've always wanted! Of course I'm going to get excited about that..." But, don't you think we should show the same kind of excitement and energy about our God?

The prophet Isaiah was really excited about God in today's verse... In fact, in the whole chapter! He's telling the people of Judah to start a special relationship with God and get excited. It's almost like he was telling these people that there was a sale. Trying to get the people all excited was a challenge... But he had a message and knew what he wanted to accomplish.

Sometimes I think we have our lives all messed up. We get excited about things that just aren't that important, but when it comes to remembering our relationship with God, we have a "ho-hum, who cares" attitude. God will always be there, so there's no rush... How wrong is that?! We need to show the same kind of excitement about God as we do when there's a great sale at our favorite store.

Day 128

{ Cain said to the Lord, "My punishment is more than I can bear. Today you are driving me from the land, and I will be hidden from your presence; I will be a restless wanderer on the earth, and whoever finds me will kill me." Genesis 4:13-14 }

Real Despair

Maggie, my dog, has lived with me for almost three years now. During that time, she has learned lots of tricks, eaten a lot of popcorn, watched a lot of TV, taken over all the furniture in my house, including my bed... She's also been punished for being bad.

When Maggie gets in trouble, she gets sent to her box. If she really gets in trouble, I close the door and leave her in there for a while. She looks out the opening... Pouting, begging silently (sometimes not so silently) to be let out... If the door is open she tries to sneak out...

Once, I sent her to the box and pushed the door closed but left it unlocked. She could have pushed it open and walked right out... Which is what I thought she would do... So I left the room. When I noticed I hadn't seen her for a while I found her still in the box! The door was still closed, and she was just waiting to be let out.

Don't sit in the box!

Why didn't the dog realize that with a push of her nose, she could go back to sleeping on the chair? I guess because the first few times I sent her to the box and closed the door she pushed on it and couldn't get out... So she was programmed to think when the door is closed -- whether it's locked or not -- she can't get out.

In Genesis, Cain is punished by God, feeling completely helpless... There's no possible way he can live. I think sometimes we all feel like that... If someone gets D's for so long... Even when they study really hard... They stop trying. Why bother?

Maybe you feel like that sometimes. I know I do. No matter what you do, something bad happens. People get sick, you don't do well in a game... You feel like God isn't there, even though you pray all the time! Don't get stuck sitting in a box with the door closed and just accept that it's locked. Work hard to make changes in your life, and eventually good stuff will happen.

Day 129

 Jesus answered, "A person who has had a bath needs only to wash his feet; his whole body is clean." John 13:10a

Singing In The Shower

I hate mornings. Maybe you're a morning person, but I just hate crawling out of my cozy bed. Just the thought of mornings makes me groan... But since mornings happen every day, there are two things I look forward to each morning... A hot shower and coffee.

There's just something about a shower that makes me feel energized. Hot water rushing out of the shower, relaxing all my muscles... Some days I could just stand under the water for 20 minutes. Not only does the shower relax and wake me up, I also get clean. A little soap and all the dirt I picked up is washed away.

But you know something? I hate wearing shoes and socks. In fact, the first thing I do when I walk in the door is lose the shoes. I usually walk around the house bare foot. Sometimes I run out to the car without shoes. At the end of every day, my feet are pretty dirty... So I wash em.

Dirt = Sin

Do you think dirt on the bottom of our feet could be like sin? When we're baptized, it's like taking a shower in the morning. We're considered clean because of Jesus' death on the cross. But we all make mistakes and mess up. It's like the dirt we get on the bottom of our feet... We don't need a whole shower again, but we do need to ask for forgiveness... Kinda like washing our feet.

Jesus took the job of washing the feet of his disciples. He was trying to make them understand that because of baptism, they were clean, but he was going to die so that the sins that happen during every day life could be forgiven and washed away.

No matter what dirt you get on the bottom of your feet during the day, you can wash it away... No matter what kind of bad thing you did during the day, it can be forgiven. So, tonight, when you get cleaned up and wash your feet, remember to ask God to forgive your sins...

Day 130

> Do not worry about what to say or how to say it. At that time you will be given what to say, for it will not be you speaking, but the Spirit of your Father speaking through you.
> Matthew 10:19-20

God Speaking Through Me

When I was in school, even though it was a Christian school, there were a lot of different groups. The "motorheads", "jocks", "snobs", "brains", "geeks", "druggies", "cheerleaders" and lots of others. As different as they were, they all had one thing in common: it wasn't cool to be a Christian in any of them.

So, here I was, a Christian kid, trying to fit in with at least one group. I knew that I should've been trying to get my friends to really be Christians instead of just claiming to be. With my friends outside of school who weren't Christians, I knew I should've invited them to church and told them more about my faith… But I was scared to.

Many times when people are faced with the opportunity to share their faith with others they use the excuse "I don't know what to say." Sometimes they're afraid of what friends will say or think of them… "Maybe they'll think I'm a loser and not want to hang out with me any more.

Putting this message in motion

It's hard to put yourself out there and take a chance. There's no way to know what friends will say, if they'll be interested or think we're crazy. I wish I could tell you that I'm confident enough to tell everyone I know about my faith… But I still worry about what people will think. I still worry about not knowing what to say.

Matthew says we shouldn't worry about what to say or how to say it because when the time comes God will be speaking through you. We should have the confidence t just walk up to people and share our faith with them… God is right there with us!

I know… It's still scary to talk to your friends about God… Especially if they aren't very religious. There's no reason to be "preachy" with them though. There are lots of ways you can introduce them to God. Have faith! The words will come out just right.

Day 131

> Dear children, let us not love with words or tongue, but with actions and in truth. 1 John 3:18

Actions vs. Words

You've probably heard the phrase "actions speak louder than words." I tell my friends if they are going to say something, they need to show they mean it instead of just saying it. So why then is our society all talk and no action? Maybe people think that others don't really care whether people stick to their word or not.

People say what others want to hear but don't follow through. I do it sometimes, maybe you do too. I'm asked to do something... Take out the garbage, do the dishes, clean up, make a phone call... Whatever... And I say I'm going to do it, but for one reason or another, I don't.

This has gotten to be such a problem that in my house, if I'm asked to do something and I say "OK, I'll do that" Jeannette expects me to not do it. She asks me over and over to do whatever I'm supposed to do. She's actually amazed if I complete the task. If I would just DO what I was supposed to do, like I said I would, life would be a lot easier.

Take a look in the mirror

I guess we're all guilty of doing this sometimes. People ask us to do something, whether it's parents, friends, teachers, neighbors... Whatever... We say we'll do something, but when it comes time to do it, we don't.

Today's verse is talking specifically about love. But doesn't this really cross over into other areas too? Isn't it showing love when we do things we're asked to do? Following through on what we say is just another way to show those around us that we love them.

I promise you that if you start following through on your statements and promises, you'll feel better (you won't be getting nagged!) and people will really listen and believe you when you say you'll do something.

Day 132

> Laughter can conceal a heavy heart; when the laughter ends, the grief remains. Proverbs 14:13

Don't Worry... Be Happy!

Some people who know me think I'm always happy. Most of the time, that's true. I'm an up-beat person who finds joy in the little things. I've always been taught that things are going to be the way they are, so you might as well be happy because being sad doesn't help.

However, I said I'm happy "most of the time". There are plenty of days where my happiness is a mask. Believe it or not, there are some days that I'm just not happy, however, most of the time nobody knows... Who wants to be around a person who's in a bad mood or sad?

Putting up "masks" goes beyond moods. Sometimes people go through the motions of being a Christian... Myself included. There are days when I pray just out of a routine, not from my heart. Or when I sit in church and think about other things, sing without emotion and worship half-heartedly.

Take action! Take off your mask

Maybe you, like me, go through the motions sometimes. Maybe you, like me, have down days. Maybe you, like me, go through times where you don't pray, sing, worship... THINK about God.

Don't worry. All of us go through these stages. We just can't let these stages become habits! Understand and accept the fact that maybe you're having a bad day or few days... Then move on!

The problem with wearing a mask is that the problem still remains. The pain or struggles are still there. To remove the masks we must take the focus off us and place it on God. Worship to express to God just what an awesome and amazing Being He is. No more pretending. No more hiding. From now on only true joy.

Day 133

> Notice the way God does things; then fall into line. Don't fight the ways of God, for who can straighten out what he has made crooked? Ecclesiastes 7:13

How To Work With God

When I read this verse, I interpret it as: "Look for where God is working and then join Him." Today's lesson is about plans. Ours and Gods... and where and why they might differ.

In my lifetime I have had many plans. I planned to be a professional baseball player... Later on, I planned to be a working drummer (and make millions of dollars!), and then I planned to have a successful business. None of those worked, but I didn't give up planning. From there, I planned a beautiful wedding with my now-wife, Jeannette. We planned everything... For August 2001.

Unfortunately, something came up and we were unable to have our wedding in August. After all that, I planned to have a successful career with a growing technology company... That didn't work out either.

Our plans may not fit God's plan

I tell you all this because, now, after all my plans have failed, I listened to what God's plan is. Work with the Youth Group at Old Paramus Reformed Church, help kids grow as Christians through these devotionals and the OPRCYouth website, go back to college, be more active in church...

So you see, sometimes our plans just don't match the plan that God has for us. I'm certain there have been times where you've had a "plan" for life that didn't work out exactly as you thought... All the planning in the world wouldn't have changed that because it wasn't what God had in mind for you!

Today is a perfect day to listen to what God is telling you. Think about your plans for the day, week, month, year and even years down the road. Do you think your plan matches God's plan for your life?

Day 134

> But if we confess our sins to him, he is faithful and just to forgive us and to cleanse us from every wrong. 1 John 1:9

Why Doesn't God Give Up On Us?

Have you ever said to yourself: "Self... I can't be a Christian anymore. I always mess up, I'm just not following God's will." Maybe you have an addiction to something, or you swear a lot, or you have a bad temper...

Sometimes it's so easy to be hard on ourselves. We're so disappointed in our behavior... We failed as Christians... AGAIN! We're really let down by the mistakes we make. Even when we try to live our life for Christ, we still mess up. After each mistake, we always find ourselves asking God to forgive us. Again... "God, how could you even think of forgiving me after I promised I'd try harder to be a better Christian?"

It's hard to imagine that even though we mess up God is ready to forgive us. We think, "Maybe God will stop listening to me if I keep messing up." When we mess up, God isn't mad at us, he doesn't stop listening... God knows what we struggle with. He knows our weaknesses. He knows the power of Satan, waiting to jump in and tempt us to make a mistake.

God never gives up!

We all feel unworthy of Gods love and forgiveness... That's because we are! But what's amazing is: God loves us and forgives us anyway! Sometimes we put "boundaries" on Gods love and forgiveness. Thinking things like "OK... I've messed up again... God could never forgive me this time..." When we do this, we're forgetting that God is in control and His grace is his to give... Not ours to take.

The next time you mess up, remember this: God loves you more than you can imagine. Jesus never said this walk would be easy. In fact, He said the exact opposite. He said it would be hard. You will face ups and downs in your faith... Regardless of whether you're up or down, God is with you and faithfully loves you through them all. Don't give up on your faith, because I promise you that God won't give up on you.

Day 135

 If you abide in Me, and My words abide in you, you will ask what you desire, and it shall be done for you. John 15:7

Minutes Are Ticking By

What is the significance of a minute in a day? What is ten minutes in a day? We each get 1440 minutes in a day and most of those go by without much notice. It can be a struggle when someone asks us what we did yesterday... It's a challenge to come up with an answer!

In the last ten minutes, 75 mothers gave birth to cute, cuddly babies that are alive and well. In those last ten minutes, 42 people said their last good-bye to the life that they lived on this earth, content or not with what they had done. For the last group of people those last ten minutes were important. The last ten minutes were important for all, actually. It takes fewer than 5 minutes from the time our hearts stop until we are in eternity.

How are you spending your day?

Most days, I can't even remember what I did an hour earlier. I go through my day, play some games, sit in classes, read books, write papers, do homework, chat on the Internet... My life is crazy! At the end of every week I look back and try to figure out what I did with all the time I had this week. What did I really accomplish?

Meeting the needs that other people have shows them that we care for them and that they are important. Each of us with a little effort has the ability to meet the needs of others. We might find we have no time to meet the needs of others because we are so busy trying to meet our own wants. You can never give too much to others, and in giving, you may just find that you meet your own needs by serving others in their needs.

Take a couple minutes today and plan out how you can serve those God placed around you by helping them get what they need. The couple of minutes that you can give to those around you today could be the biggest difference anyone has made in their life. And could be the best few minutes of your day, too.

Day 136

> Therefore confess your sins to each other and pray for each other so that you may be healed. The prayer of a righteous man is powerful and effective. John 5:16

Who Can You Talk To?

Sometimes it's hard to know who to talk to. Maybe you need someone to talk to about struggles you're facing. Maybe you need to talk to someone about something personal... Either way, you don't want it blabbed all over church, school and home.

Today's Bible verse encourages us to talk to other Christians and build each other up... Sometimes though, our options for people to talk to are limited.

Some people think church is a place where everyone goes to be happy and cheerful and act perfect. Of course we all know that Christians aren't any more perfect than anyone else. We don't always have easy lives or easy decisions to make... In fact, sometimes being a Christian makes things harder!

So who can you talk to?

Church gossip can be worse than the politics are in congress, but we don't have to go along with it. If you pretend nothing is wrong because you don't trust the other people at church, you're not giving the majority of churchgoers a fair chance. The bible tells us to admit our faults to others and seek encouragement from each other. But if you are in an environment where gossip spreads fast, you want to be very careful about who you do talk to. It's important to find someone who you can look up to in Christ, someone who is actually living a Christian life, not just putting on a Christian suit when they go to church. Try to find out how they live their life outside of church. When you are truly living a life to please God, it's really easy to see when others are too.

If you are having a hard time figuring out who you can talk to, chat with a church official. There may be some exceptions, but for the most part, they are very good to talk to.

Look around your church and ask yourself, if someone else is having a problem, do I live a life that would invite them to bring their problems to me?

Day 137

 Our bodies now disappoint us, but when they are raised, they will be full of glory. They are weak now, but when they are raised, they will be full of power. They are natural human bodies now, but when they are raised, they will be spiritual bodies. For just as there are natural bodies, so also there are spiritual bodies. 1 Corinthians 15:43-44

What Is Perfection?

Every day I get out of bed and go through my morning rituals... Some days I look in the mirror and see a smile looking back at me... Most days I don't like the reflection I see. What I'd like to see is a tall, thin, blonde man with perfect hair, teeth, and smile. I'd like to see someone thin with 6-pack abs, muscles and a small waist.

We all struggle with our physical image and appearance. I battle with being over weight (those of you who know me might think I'm losing the battle!)... I have terrible hair, my face is round, and I wear glasses... I'm sure we all have things we would change if we could. The reflection we see isn't what we wish for...

What do you see in the mirror?

You look in the mirror and you can probably tell me more about you that you don't like than what you do. Maybe you're underweight or overweight. Maybe you're too tall or too short. Maybe you have acne or other blemishes. Maybe you have birthmarks or deformities. Whatever you see in that mirror, I promise you're not the only one who would change stuff about the way they look.

The fact is it won't always be this way. In the course of your earthly life you will probably change a lot! You may grow taller and your skin may grow wrinkly. Then you may even grow shorter. But, when you leave this earth, we are promised, that our bodies will look so much better.

So, I want to encourage you... No matter what you may find wrong with your body now (which, I remind you is perfect to God), it will go away someday. You have hope. You will be more beautiful than any of us can imagine. Let that fill you will hope when you look into your reflection!

Day 138

> Like a city whose walls are broken down is a man who lacks self-control. Proverbs 25:28

One More Chip

Imagine a city with no walls and no defenses. The ruler of the city has neglected to build safer walls and a bigger army thinking, "tomorrow is another day." The next day arrives, and again the ruler neglects the need. Suddenly, thousands of enemy soldiers come over the horizon and attack the city. The ruler realizes that he is the reason for the doom of his city.

In this example, perhaps the ruler should have exercised a little self-control. Perhaps he was so busy doing things that weren't important... But were more enjoyable... That he neglected what was really important.

A Christian with no self-control is just like this ruler. Without self-control, the devil can attack at any time, with any temptation he pleases, causing you to be torn between God and sin. He will make you ineffective, with the eventual goal of stealing your joy, killing your Christian spirit, and totally destroying your life.

Self-control stinks...

I'll be the first to admit that self-control stinks... All the things that seem like fun (or taste good or feel good) may not be the best things for us... But... We must learn to control ourselves, to not give in to every urge whatever it may be; not just knowing what is right, but doing it. Without self-control, we become ineffective, and God has no place for an ineffective servant in His kingdom.

When I'm struggling with self-control, I always try to pray. I know when what I'm doing is wrong... So I pray for God to give me the strength to get through the battle. Because I know, in the end, that God will help me realize there are other things that I should be doing that are far more important.

The key to gaining self-control is prayer. When you pray for help, you'll learn to win the battles of what you want to do vs. what you know you should do. They don't use the slogan, "Can't eat just one" for nothing – they know people lack self-control.

Day 139

> All Scripture is God-breathed and is useful for teaching, rebuking, correcting and training in righteousness so that the man of God may be thoroughly equipped for every good work.
> 2 Timothy 3:16-17

The Ultimate Script

Sometimes I question whether or not the Bible is fact or fiction. I mean, the stories all seem so... I don't know... Too good to be true. The more I read and study, the more I question. Is this really written by God? Or just the work of a genius writer?

Many people have questioned whether the bible was truly accurate. How do we know it's really the truth? The bible was written over a 1500-year period, by over 40 different authors and in different languages. Without any contradiction of ideas.

Time after time, people have tried to disprove events that the bible talks about only to find that the event did actually occur. A scientist who was trying to disprove it wrote one of the most compelling books written about the Death, Burial and resurrection and the evidence he found led him to believe and brought him to Jesus.

Fact or fiction?

No human could have come up with this stuff on his own. With our human nature we would create gods that are powerful and don't put up with people messing up. We wouldn't create a God of grace, but one of power. Take a look at some religions that are considered cults, you'll find that the gods they worship are something that a human would have invented.

The more I study the more I believe the Bible is 100% true and 100% inspired by God. The Bible was written by a God who is more amazing than we could ever imagine. Have you ever been reading a Bible verse when all of a sudden it took on a new meaning? It happens all the time, it's because God's word is alive.

It's natural to question the Bible, don't accept what other people say about it without really digging in and learning for yourself. When you seek God's face and dig into the Bible for His guidance, you'll find it's much more alive than you've ever seen before.

Day 140

> Brothers, I do not consider myself yet to have taken hold of it. But one thing I do: Forgetting what is behind and straining toward what is ahead, I press on toward the goal to win the prize for which God has called me heavenward in Christ Jesus. Philippians 3:13-14

If At First You Don't Succeed...

Some of you may not know this about me: I have started about 25 businesses in my adult life. They were all based on great ideas or products. Some of them were moderately successful, some of them didn't even make $1

There are a variety of reasons why some of these businesses flopped. Bad timing, improper planning, lack of funding... The list goes on and on. And so do my ideas!

I tell you this because all the businesses you hear about and all the products you use were started by someone who had great ideas that flopped before finding the ONE that worked. Thomas Edison (the light bulb guy...) tried over 900 times before his great idea actually worked. If his life was anything like mine, his wife must have thought he was crazy to keep trying!

Try something Other than sky-diving

We have all dealt with failure and depression. Some of us before we ever find any type of success. The problem is that we let these failures and our past lead to emotions, the emotions lead to depression, and the depression lead to a victory for Satan.

The solution is quite easy to talk about, but can be quite difficult to put into practice in our lives. We need to forget about our past and keep looking ahead. Paul (The guy who wrote Philippians) did. Even though he had his faults, blunders, and failures, he forgot about the past and stayed totally committed to Christ.

My dream was to work with young people. After years of searching for a business that could make me happy, I found it just waiting for me... And I've had a taste of success... You're reading this message and maybe it will help you get through your day. Maybe it will encourage you to get closer to God. Being a Christian helps us learn from our mistakes, dust off our clothes and reach for another dream.

Day 141

{ Whatever exists has already been named, and what man is has been known; no man can contend with one who is stronger than he. Ecclesiastes 6:10 }

Out Of Control? Me Too!

Ok... How bout that verse in English? Here it is... You can't argue with God about the future. No matter how hard you try, there's a plan in place and you're just along for the ride.

Let me share my experience with you. Briefly... I promise. When I was 16 everyone said I should be a teacher or be in some field where I could work with kids. I absolutely loved hanging with young people. I coached softball and did a lot of things with the youth in my church and community.

Somehow I just couldn't see myself in school for the rest of my life... I couldn't wait to get OUT of school, why would I want to work there? Besides. I knew better. I didn't want to go to college, just wanted to run a business and make lots of money.

Don't fool yourself

I tried a lot of things, none of them really worked out, and people always kept nagging me: you should be working with young people in some way. Even though I always thought maybe I would like to do that, I never felt I was good at it, never thought it would work out. Always had excuses for why I should try other things instead.

After I lost my job, I woke up one morning and said to myself... "Self! Wake up! It's time you did what you should have been doing all along. Look into working with young people." I got up, started looking into college programs, talked to the Pastor at my church to get his input and jumped in with both feet.

I'm not saying you should know right this second what you want to do with your life. I didn't figure it out until I was 30. I'm just telling you that God has a plan. He has it all figured out and no matter what you think you know, God knows better. Don't wait until your old like me to realize that God has a plan for you.

Day 142

> For God did not give us a spirit of timidity, but a spirit of power, of love and of self-discipline. 2 Timothy 1:7

Decisions, Decisions

When I read the word "timid" in today's verse, I think apprehension, fear, nervous. I don't know about you, but all these words leave me feeling pretty bad. They make me feel exhausted and negative. I believe God wants us to feel His love and power which helps us gain self-discipline.

God gave us strong minds with the ability to know right from wrong. We have the ability to make decisions, both good and bad. Some of them are meaningless, some impact the rest of our lives! This whole ability to make decisions starts when we're babies and gradually gets harder and harder as we grow up.

Eventually our decisions impact more than just us. I can tell you that I have made good and bad decisions that I thought would only affect me, but later on had an impact on those that I love too! I'm sure you've had similar experiences in your life.

Think before deciding

We all need to be so careful when making decisions... Especially emotional decisions. Emotions at times seem to get in the way of the decision making process. We get carried away and let our feelings of anger, love, frustration... Whatever... Make the decision we're making seem like a good one. Maybe the only one. When there are actually lots of options.

Self-discipline helps us make decisions. It's something that we gain as we get older. We need to fill our hearts and minds with things that can help our sprit grow. Only allow truth to dwell in your mind. Ward off all thoughts of evil and fear. And when evil and fear enter, know that they were not given by God and ask God to take them away.

Asking God to guide you in your decisions will help you do the right things that will take you down the right path in life.

Day 143

 Answer me when I call to you, O my righteous God.
Psalm 4:1a

Is There Anyone Out There?

Have you ever been lost? I have. When I was young I wandered off toward something that seemed interesting. Looking back, it wasn't such a good idea, but at the time, it looked like fun!

I was around 5 and had walked in to a hallway filled with big sponge balls (like those pits at the amusement parks)... I was wandering around in a maze. I was walking around in circles. One wrong turn after another left me completely confused and afraid.

My dad, had a clear view of me and which way I should be going, but because of the way the maze was constructed, I couldn't see him... But I could hear his voice. I could hear his voice giving me directions. Sometimes I got so frustrated by the whole thing I just sat still and cried. Every time I freaked out, the voice of my dad made me continue walking.

Have some faith!

How many times have we, as Christians, been in this same situation? How many times have you cried out to God asking to come and save you? We get stuck and have no idea which way to turn. Sometimes it seems as if God abandoned us, but if we listen, he's actually guiding us through the maze.

We need to trust and follow Him... Even though we can't see Him. God loves us, even when we yell at Him for not just helping us out right away. As if that is not comfort enough... Imagine what it will be like when we get to the end! We can run to Him and know that we are finally safe from all of the evils in this world.

Are you stuck in the middle of the maze? Don't forget God hears all your prayers. He sees your tears. He knows all of your fears. He is gently guiding you through the maze. All you have to do is listen.

Day 144

> Cast your cares on the Lord and he will sustain you; he will never let the righteous fall. Psalms 55:22

Please Hold

You may be a little young to really be annoyed by the words "Please Hold". Our lives today are a blur. We're on the phone, talking, solving problems, looking for information... If you haven't already gotten tired of these simple words, you soon will... I promise.

About every call I make starts with a phrase like, "Thanks for calling XYZ Company... Please hold..." or how about voicemail: "Hi, you've reached Joel... I can't take your call, so leave a message..." Blah Blah Blah... I hope you're never in need of immediate help because you'll need a miracle to get someone to actually pick up the phone!

Direct connection

As Christians, we have a direct link... Someone who'll pick up our call right when we need them... God... Prayer is a powerful thing. I could make a list a mile long of prayers that were answered, and an even longer list of people who felt better about their situation after they prayed.

I had the privilege to know some very special people... Extreme Christians. They happened to be my aunt and uncle. These people had NOTHING to be happy about. She was extremely ill for 40 years. The funny thing about them is that what I remember isn't that she was sick, but that they prayed every day about their situation. Not to help her feel better... To help them reach others and thank God for the blessings they were given.

Prayer isn't just for people who are sick. Prayer is the perfect connection to God... For every situation... We can praise God, ask him to watch over us, help us through a tough situation... We can ask God for advice, for safety... You can talk to God about anything! Get in the habit of using that direct connection to God. I promise you'll feel better about life if you pray. And you'll never hear, "Please hold" or get transferred from one person to the next. God is there waiting for your call.

Day 145

> Therefore, if anyone is in Christ, he is a new creation; the old has gone, the new has come! 2 Corinthians 5:17

Butterflies

Butterflies? You think I've finally lost it (go ahead... admit it)... What could Butterflies have to do with anything?

Think about it for a second... Butterflies come from where? Caterpillars... Pretty ugly creatures, if you ask me. They inch along, slowly going about their business. Then, as hard as it is to believe, they build a cocoon... An even UGLIER home for themselves.

As time goes on, they start moving around in their little homes and begin peeking out... When they finally get out, they sit on a branch and stretch their wings... All of a sudden they start flying... They're beautiful!

Christians are like butterflies

We are, by nature, sinful. If we're talking spiritually, we're pretty gross and ugly. We kinda move through life slowly, maybe without purpose similar to a caterpillar. All of a sudden we "see the light". Some of our cocoons are built by experiencing God's love through others. Others are built to shelter us from bad things. Either way, we become more open to God's love.

In that secret place God helps our hearts develop and open until we can see him. Then, there is a battle of wills, spiritual warfare. God wants us with Him in the light, Satan doesn't. The fight continues and eventually we break free and go with God. We sit in the newfound light and stretch our wings. We grow in Christ, until one day, we fly. We soar in Christ and experience his joy. Then, when we are fully rooted in him, he sets us free to go into this world and show others His light. Caterpillars don't have it easy and becoming a butterfly is hard work. But the beauty that comes after the transformation is incredible! No matter where you are in your journey, remember that you are God's little butterfly, and He has amazing plans for you!

And you didn't think I could make sense of that... Shame on you.

Day 146

{ Don't let anyone look down on you because you are young, but set an example for the believers in speech, in life, in love, in faith and in purity. 1 Timothy 4:12 }

Be An Example

Sometimes, as young people, we might feel like we can't make a difference in a community or church. Sometimes everyone goes about their business, talking about how they're doing work for the church or how they've made an impression on someone else's life.

I happen to think that young people can make a huge difference in the lives of people and in a church or community. We have lots of energy and enthusiasm... That goes a long way!

So why don't more people listen to us? Why don't people notice when we do good things? Why don't people think we can be good Christians? Why? Why? Why?

Be an example today...

The answer is... They do. People do all of those things. They listen, notice and think we can be very good Christians... We're just too busy being kids to notice them noticing!

Can you think of five ways young people can be good Christians and set an example for others? You could help others... Maybe elderly people by doing lawn work or painting a building... Visit people from church who aren't able to get out... You could even send cards to those people -- they LOVE knowing you're thinking of them. You could do work for a food drive or homeless shelter.

There are opportunities everywhere to set a good example for other young people AND for adults! You can make a difference in your church and community!

Just think, "I'll be an example today in speech by not swearing; in life by doing what pleases God; in love by caring about others; in faith by praying and worshiping God; and in purity by choosing what's right." Be an example today!

Day 147

{ You shall have no other gods before me. Exodus 20:3 }

Are The Things You Like Bad?

Hopefully this sounds familiar to you. It's one of the 10 Commandments. Sometimes I think we hear them so often that we forget how important they are... Or worse, we hear them, but don't understand them.

I was reading through Exodus today, specifically chapter 20 where the Commandments are listed. Sometimes I think the Bible wasn't written for today's world, but it really is...

When these Commandments were given to Moses, they were meant to be taken literally. The Israelites were worshipping other gods... The sun god, rain god, etc. And the true God was telling them they shouldn't believe in anyone but Him.

So... What does that have to do with today?

Today, we don't really worship other gods or idols in the same sense as the Israelites did, but think about this for a second. Could other things be considered gods? I'm not saying they are or aren't, but just think about it in your life.

Maybe you place too much emphasis on clothing... Stereos, jewelry or other possessions. It's one thing to be excited about having them... But at what point does your enthusiasm go too far? Do you think those things could be considered gods?

I've seen a lot of people "worship" cars... Maybe expensive sports cars or other luxury cars. I've seen people really place too much emphasis on jewelry and other things. I'm not saying that if you like these items you're breaking one of the commandments. I'm just asking you to think about your feelings about these material things and make sure you have a healthy appreciation for them and realize that you need to be 100% committed to the one TRUE God.

Day 148

> For we are God's workmanship, created in Christ Jesus to do good works, which God prepared in advance for us to do.
> Ephesians 2:10

It's Good To Be You

I know of some people, both young and old, who don't think much of themselves. They always had the feeling that they weren't good enough for anyone to love, could never measure up to their parents expectations, and felt like everyone in their lives had given up on them.

No matter what they achieved, it always seemed like it just wasn't good enough. Maybe in school... No matter how hard they worked and what grades they got, when report card day came, it wasn't good enough for their parents. In sports, no matter how many hits they got in a game, someone would come along and say something like, "Wow... Only one more hit and you would have had a perfect game!"

Maybe you or someone you know struggles with these same feelings. When I was younger I certainly did. My parents were very loving, that wasn't my issue, but I always felt like I wasn't as important as other people. Teachers didn't pay much attention to me, coach's always picked other kids to do stuff, people at church didn't pay much attention to my talents or interests...

You're God's creation!

He has a plan for you. He created you with that in mind! You have a purpose for being here on this earth. He saw all your mistakes and all the joy you would find. He created you, knowing you better than you know yourself!

Sometimes it's hard to remember that, especially when we're feeling a little down, or are struggling with a certain issue... It's hard to remember that we're part of a big puzzle and everything we do has a purpose...

God has a purpose for your life. He had a plan long before you were even born... So the next time you feel like you don't measure up or you start to feel like you don't matter to those around you, just remember that He has an incredible plan for you... Let that thought and the love that comes with it be in the front of your mind.

Day 149

> And now these three remain: faith, hope and love. But the greatest of these is love. 1 Corinthians 13:13

Love Is In The Air

Every morning, I get up and tell Jeannette I love her. Every morning, I get up and tell Maggie I love her. Every morning, I get up and love my first cup of coffee. Through the day, I love TV shows, songs, movies, types of cars, jokes, and lots of other stuff.

Who and what do you love? Your family? Pets? Boyfriend or girlfriend? Friends? Things? How about God? Each of these is a different "level" of love. You obviously love your family differently than you love your dog. And your friends differently than a movie.

Love: a powerful emotion

God, the creator of love, wants us to know that loving Him is the first and greatest commandment he gives us. "Jesus replied: 'Love the Lord your God with all your heart and with all your soul and with all your mind. This is the first and greatest commandment. And the second is like it: Love your neighbor as yourself. All the Law and the Prophets hang on these two commandments.'" (Matthew 22:37-40).

Gods love for us is true unconditional love; the closest, I think, humans come to that type of love is the love, that a parent has for their child. God understands the strong feelings and commitment that a parent has for their child but he insists that we love him even above our children, even asking Abraham to sacrifice his only son, Isaac.

Pretty amazing, huh? We're told to love God above everything else! More than our favorite teams, sports, cars, people, pets... More than everything and everyone in our life... Do you always do that?

Love is a very powerful emotion and we need to keep this emotion focused on God. As you begin dating and even when you find the person you intend to marry; be sure that your love for God remains true, strong, first and foremost in your life.

Day 150

{ Do not envy wicked men, do not desire their company; for their hearts plot violence, and their lips talk about making trouble. Proverbs 24:1-2 }

Wealth Doesn't Equal Happiness

I have a secret to share with you today. I'm not proud of it, but sometimes I wish my life was more like someone famous. Maybe you have the same thoughts... Wonder what it would be like to switch places with someone famous for a day.

What would it be like to be a professional athlete? Movie star? Musician? To have so much money you couldn't spend it all... To be able to buy anything and everything... Nice cars, nice clothes, live in huge houses... Go shopping all the time... That would be a great life, don't you think?

Lately though, I've been noticing that their lives aren't always so great. Sure... They have money and power, but I keep watching them go through divorces, battle with drugs and sometimes lose everything. They have problems with the police, get in lots of fights, people following them around... Maybe I don't want their lives after all.

Choose your role models carefully

There are people who have a lot of money and fame and are Christians! People like President Bush, Kurt Warner and lots of other people have accumulated great wealth while making good Christian decisions. Now those are role models. They have it all, stay out of trouble, help others and do lots of good things for communities!

The author of today's verse felt so strongly about the danger of imitating the wrong kind of people because he was sure that it would be hard to be faithful to God with the temptations that fame and fortune can bring. He knew that our nature would be to compare our lives to those famous people and try to be like them...

Are you like me? Are you occasionally guilty of wondering what it would be like to be rich or famous? If so, Proverbs tells you that if you know the Lord, you are already richer than you could possibly be with all the money or possessions in the world. Learn about people who have it all and try to do the right thing...

Day 151

> Trust in the Lord with all your heart and lean not on your own understanding; in all your ways acknowledge him, and he will make your paths straight. Proverbs 3:5-6

Be Patient

So... You pray to God to help you with a problem or issue in your life. You really need an answer... Now... It seems like God is ignoring you. You start getting discouraged. Today's verse tells us what the next step should be -- trust God with all your heart.

I'm guilty of doing this... "God," I pray, "Please, please help me decide what to do. I need to know if I should start this new study group at church. I'd like to start tomorrow, so if you have a chance, God, please let me know today if I should go ahead with it or try something else." Sound familiar?

We tire of waiting for God... We want an answer to our prayers now! It's hard to trust and be patient. It's easier to trust in our own abilities than to trust God when He doesn't seem to be coming through for us. As our faith grows we learn to trust God.

Patience is a virtue

What can you do with unanswered prayer in your life? Choose faith in God; let Him show you the answer He has for you. Recognize that your timing might be a bit different than God's and that His answer might not be the one you were expecting.

It's hard to wait. We have all these great ideas, and we want God's blessing. But we're anxious to go now! We're so sure we have it all figured out. Know exactly what we're supposed to do... And God waits... And waits... Sometimes he comes through with the answer we were hoping for, sometimes he says, "You know what? I think you should try this instead..."

Time sometimes seems like too great a cost for an answer from God. Grow in the knowledge of Jesus Christ! Trust Him for your unanswered prayers. He will be faithful!

Day 152

{ I know your deeds, that you are neither cold nor hot. I wish you were either one or the other! So, because you are lukewarm -- neither hot nor cold -- I am about to spit you out of my mouth. Revelation 3:15-16 }

Cold, Hot, or Lukewarm?

Have you ever heard the phrase "walking the fence"? Sometimes people use this phrase to describe someone who can't make a decision or who can't live a certain lifestyle completely.

We have a hard time making decisions. There are so many choices for everything! We can't decide if we want pizza or burgers; whether we want to go to the mall or to the outlet stores. When there are so many choices, we want to be so sure that we make the right one that we don't make any!

Everyone at one time or another has tried to keep his balance while "walking on a fence". Sometimes we make it and sometimes we fall. When it comes to Christianity, far too many people try to "walk the fence." They keep one foot in the Spirit while one foot flirts with the world. These are some of the unhappiest people in the world.

So... What's your temperature?

Think about the word lukewarm. How would you describe it? I'd say, "Not hot, not cold" – if I was referring to water coming out of a faucet, I'd mean that both the hot and cold water was turned on equally. If I was washing dishes, that wouldn't be the best water to do it in... I'd want to use hot water... Right?

Are you a "lukewarm Christian"? Or are really hot... Just think about your life on a daily basis. Are you the kind of person that really strives to be obedient to God and follow the path of Jesus? Or are you content to say and do the right things on Sundays and live a different life Monday through Saturday.

If God is God and Christ is our Savior, we need to give our complete attention and whole heart to God. A lukewarm Christian will never have the joy of knowing the fullness of God. Obedience is the key to real faith. This is real faith: believing and acting obediently regardless of what's happening around us.

Day 153

> Even a child is known by his actions, by whether his conduct is pure and right. Proverbs 20:11

Reputations

Reputation: What people think of someone because of their attitude, actions or words.

Eminem, Britney Spears, Madonna, 50 Cent, Kobe Bryant, cheerleaders, athletes and politicians. What do all these people have in common? Famous? Rich? Celebrities? Talented? Attractive?

Those things are all true, but they also all have reputations. Some of those people have good reputations, some not. But, whether individuals or groups of people, everyone in that list has earned a reputation. Violent, tough, innocent, exotic, squeaky clean, fun, friendly, liars...

What's your reputation?

In most cases you build and earn a reputation, either good or bad, by doing things more than once. You wouldn't earn a reputation of being smart if you got one "A" on a homework assignment, but you might be if you got straight "A's" on your report card. Once could have been lucky... It's repeating a certain behavior that earns you a reputation.

You can earn a reputation as a Christian by doing little things: helping someone carry books when they're struggling, helping someone with homework, staying out of trouble at school, not drinking beer or smoking, going to youth group... There are so many ways to build a good reputation.

Spend some time thinking about what your reputation is and what you have done to earn that... Do you think it's a fair reputation? Accurate? Did you earn it? Do you like it? Hate it? Would you keep your reputation or change it? If you find you don't like the one you have, it's not too late to change it! Take action and earn a good reputation as a Christian.

Day 154

> Dear friends, let us love one another, for love comes from God. Everyone who lives has been born of God and knows God. Whoever does not love does not know God because God is love. 1 John 4:7-8

Kiss A Frog

Sometimes I feel like a frog... Do you? Frogs feel slow, ugly, droopy and as if that isn't bad enough, they're green. I feel like that when I want to care but don't, I want to be smart but feel dumb, when I want to be thankful for something but instead am full of resent, when I want to share with others but am actually selfish.

Maybe you remember the story of the prince who was turned into a frog by a wicked witch. He looked and felt like a frog, but really wasn't. Only the kiss of a beautiful girl could change him back... Only one problem with that... How many girls do you know who go around kissing frogs?

Of course, miracles do happen... There sat the frog, waiting to be kissed... And along comes a beautiful girl (with too much time on her hands) and for whatever reason, she decides to give the frog a kiss... Of course, you know what happens.. The frog turns into a handsome prince and they live happily ever after!

Save a prince or princess!

OK... So you aren't going to go around kissing frogs... It's a fairytale... But... You can make a difference in someone's life! Helping God make changes in people is an incredible feeling!

Think about how many people you know... I bet you influence more people than you'd ever imagine! What about teachers? Friends? People you see at the store all the time? Anyone you say hello to as you're walking through your day is someone that you could make feel better! You can help people begin changing by doing simple things like praying for them or bringing them to youth group activities or to church...

You have the power to help people who may feel like frogs turn into princes or princesses! Think about the people in your life who have the potential to be a prince or princess... Kiss a frog... Make a difference in someone's life!

Day 155

> But as for me, it is good to be near God. I have made the Sovereign Lord my refuge; I will tell of all your deeds.
> Psalm 73:28

I Need A Break

Have you ever had "one of those days" – you know the ones... Where there is so much stuff you need to get done and can't seem to get any of it accomplished? Every day is "one of those days" for me. From the moment I get up until the moment I go to sleep there is something that I should be doing. And it never gets completely done.

I know that you're busy... Just like me. Some weeks are busier than others. Depending on the week, I have Sunday school lessons to prepare, youth group nights to plan, special events to plan, schoolwork...

I'm sure you have days and weeks like that too! In fact, I'm sure you have worse weeks than me... Maybe you're dealing with relatives who are really sick or a divorce in your family or something else along with all your schoolwork and sports and everything else that you have to do...

Shelter from the craziness!

In my life, sometimes I need a break... A shelter... Quiet time. I tell Jeannette that I just need to get away for a few hours. No phone, no dog, no people bugging me, no schoolbooks, no computer... Just quiet time to get away from the craziness...

Often when I get away for a while I spend time praying. I go for a walk or lock myself in a room or go for a drive or to some other quiet place. I talk to God about all the stuff going on in my life. All the stresses and things demanding my attention. I ask him why things happen to my family or me... I talk to him about all my frustrations... He is my shelter!

Are you hurting inside? Stressing over school, parents, friends, work... Or anything else in your life? Are you searching a break from those stresses?? Looking for a shelter? Turn to God. He will be your shelter. He loves you and he longs for your presence even more than you long for His.

Day 156

{ The Lord delights in those who fear him, who put their hope in his unfailing love. Psalm 147:11 }

Trust Me

You've heard a lot about my dog, Maggie. A family rescued her so she wouldn't have to live on the streets... But they couldn't keep her any more. Maggie had bounced from home to home, never really getting comfortable with the people she was with.

Because Maggie bounced from home to home, it took some time for her to trust us. She was nervous when anyone raised their voice, she wasn't sure of what her new routine was going to be...

Today Maggie trusts us to take care of everything for her. She knows that when she's hungry we'll feed her (or give her treats!) and when she needs to go outside, someone will go out with her. When she lays with us on the sofa, she stretches out on her back, paws up in the air, and looks at us until we pet her. Being on her back is a vulnerable position so she must really trust us.

Who do you trust?

Today's verse tells us that the Lord delights in those who put their hope in his unfailing love. Doesn't it feel good when someone trusts you with something important? Imagine how God feels when we trust Him completely. When we put our hope in His unfailing love, we trust that He wants the best for our lives.

Trusting God completely means believing that He'll always be there for us. When we call to Him for help, he doesn't respond with, "Now what?" He loved it when we ask for help.

How are you doing at trusting the Lord with your life? What challenges do you face today? Are you scared of anything coming up? Your trust in God also shows that your hope is in Him. You're trusting that He will protect you through the dangers or challenges in your life. By respecting God's plan and putting your hope in Him, you demonstrate trust in Him to be the Lord of your life.

Day 157

 Therefore, if you are offering your gift at the altar and there remember that your brother has something against you, leave your gift there in front of the altar. First go and be reconciled to your brother; then come and offer your gift.
Matthew 5:23-24

You Talkin' To Me?

In my life there have been so many frustrations, fights and problems with friends, that I couldn't even begin to tell you about them. Times when I had arguments with even my best friends... And didn't talk to them for weeks or months; sometimes never again!

Sometimes we get into situations where we have problems with friends. If you're like me, maybe you stop talking to them thinking they'll ask you what's wrong... Maybe you lock yourself in your room and cry about what's going on...

Maybe, when you have a problem with someone you start circulating stories about them or start making harsh smart-mouthed comments... Maybe you just run away when you have to deal with a situation or person. Everyone solves conflicts and problems differently.

How do you solve conflicts?

How do you fix a problem with a friend or family member? Do you handle the situation in a positive way? I'm sure there are times when you handle the situation perfectly, and other times when you could do things differently. If you do any of the things mentioned above you may be hurting your relationship more. The problem isn't going to go away because you're avoiding it.

Even though you want to place blame, being right or wrong doesn't really matter. Our verse today says you are the one who has to make peace with your brother before worshiping God. You should start fixing the problem right away. The longer a problem goes unfixed the harder it is to solve.

Friendships and family relationships are a gift from God, far too important to let go of without working to fix them. Be the bigger person... Make the first move, you will be glad you did. Forgiving someone is one of the best gifts you can give to yourself.

Day 158

 Be joyful always; pray continually; give thanks in all circumstances, for this is God's will for you in Christ Jesus.
1 Thessalonians 5:16-18

Powerful Four-Letter Word

Maybe you remember the "I Love You" e-mail virus... It spread like crazy because everyone wanted to read a message with that subject. Maybe you remember the movie "You've Got Mail"... There was a line in that movie where Tom Hanks said to Meg Ryan something like... "You've got mail... Those are powerful words."

I don't know about you, but I check e-mail first thing in the morning, hoping to hear from loved ones... Maybe from Jeannette, from my loving church partners, friends, kids from church groups or other people I talk to. There isn't much I do in the morning before checking e-mail (other than take a shower and get my coffee!). Being wanted and loved is such an important emotion ... I'll take it any way I can get it!

Maybe you don't check your e-mail first thing... Maybe it's the phone call from your boyfriend or girlfriend... Or the regular mail... Regardless, we're all looking for that message from our loved ones that will carry us through the rest of the day. In fact, sometimes I wish so much for that e-mail all I can think about is when one of those people will contact me again.

Waiting for love

If we get caught up waiting to hear from loved ones, do you think God feels that way? I think we were put on this earth to glorify and love God.

Sometimes I wonder if God is waiting for our words of love. Do you think He waits impatiently in Heaven wondering when we'll take a second to say hello and tell Him how much we love Him?

Just think about the last time you rushed home to check your e-mail or ran past a family member to answer the phone... If we do that, imagine how our Heavenly Father feels at the thought of hearing from us! Take time to pray today. Take time to thank God for the day and for loving you.

Day 159

 When tempted, no one should say, "God is tempting me." For God cannot be tempted by evil, nor does he tempt anyone. Every good and perfect gift is from above, coming down from the Father of the heavenly lights who does not change like shifting shadows. James 1:13, 17

Temptation Island

We live in a world where temptation is everywhere. Every day on TV we see images that are tempting. The media plays right in to it all with programs that encourage couples to split up and choose other partners shows that the contestants need to lie, cheat, and scheme to win.

We all struggle with temptation... Why do we need to see it on TV or hear about it on the radio? Isn't that just adding to our thought that temptation is something to give in to? That's really the object of these games, I think... To see who'll give in to temptation first... And that just reinforces the idea that we'll eventually give in too.

One thing I hear often is, "Why is God tempting me by putting me in this situation?" Maybe you've asked this question... I know I have.

Temptations vs. Gifts

I have a new perspective on temptations. I can no longer blame God for tempting me with various things, putting this in my life that really test my weaknesses... And neither should you. Because God only gives us good and perfect gifts.

Gift (noun): Something given; voluntarily without compensation. (Webster's Dictionary)

In other words, giving something without expecting anything in return. How often have you done that? But God gives good and perfect gifts without wanting anything in return.

So remember, the next time you face temptation, remember that it isn't coming from God, For God cannot be tempted by evil, nor does he tempt anyone. But instead gives us good and perfect gifts. Beware of Satan who is always trying to get us to give in to temptation... Temptation doesn't automatically mean we're going to be weak and give in like in the TV shows... Be strong!

Day 160

> The heavens declare the glory of God; the skies proclaim the work of his hands. Psalm 19:1

Stop And Smell The Roses

It isn't often that I take a look out my window and say, "Wow... That is really beautiful!" Not because there isn't anything beautiful outside my window, but because I'm always so busy that I don't take the time to notice these things...

We live in a pretty amazing world. One thing that I find especially cool is that everywhere I've visited, there was something that I found especially beautiful.

In Michigan, there's the Great Lakes... In Georgia, beautiful trees and lush lawns... In Florida, gorgeous weather... In the Bahamas the water was so clear it was like looking through a clear window and the flowers and trees were unlike anything I have ever seen... In New Jersey... Well, I'm sure there's something beautiful here too... Come on... We've all heard the jokes...

Take five

Maybe you've heard the phrase "Stop and smell the roses"... Sometimes we get so busy doing things -- sports games and practices, school plays, parties, schoolwork -- that we forget to see the beauty in the things around us... In other words... We don't "take time to smell the roses"...

When you're out doing stuff do you see the beauty around you? Do you think about God's power and the perfectness of creation? I bet that like me, most of the time you're in such a hurry that you don't take the time to look around and take note of all the beautiful things God has created.

Everywhere you go there are beautiful things for us to enjoy... Take 5 minutes out of every day to enjoy God's work. It'll be the most amazing 5 minutes of the day. A time for you to stop running and quietly connect with God. An opportunity for you to praise God for creating this amazing world and to thank him for giving you the opportunity to stop and smell the roses.

Day 161

 Then he called the crowd to him along with his disciples and said: "If anyone would come after me, he must deny himself and take up his cross and follow me. For whoever wants to save his life will lose it, but whoever loses his life for me and for the gospel will save it. What good is it for a man to gain the whole world, yet forfeit his soul? Mark 8:34-36

Help Wanted

Job description: hard work, long hours, low pay... But the long-term benefits are out of this world! Apply within.

I know what you're thinking: Sounds great, huh? Where do I sign up for that job?

OK, so I'm being sarcastic... I can't remember the last time I heard of someone reading through the "help wanted" section of a paper and getting excited about taking a job that didn't pay well. We're programmed to do things that will make us a lot of money and give us the option to buy everything we want!

The cost of discipleship

To take up the cross and follow Jesus means to be willing to do anything and go anywhere for your Lord. When you 'pick up the cross and follow' you're saying you want God to work in and through you. That you're ready to let your light shine and tell and show everyone in your life that you're a Christian, and you want to explain to them how great it is!

I personally worked in "Corporate America" ... I tried climbing the corporate ladder... To be successful, get ahead and make lots of money... But I found out my ladder was leaning against the wrong building! I've been wasting my time... That wasn't what God had in mind for me but I was so busy looking for the perfect job that I missed the job that was created just for me!

Don't waste your time today or any day... God is right there with you, ready to guide you to a more meaningful life: to be a disciple. Being a disciple is to pursue Jesus with extreme passion... Be Christ-like in your every thought and word.

Day 162

> What good is it for a man to gain the whole world, yet forfeit his soul? Mark 8:36

Go Do Something!

Two things are certain in life: birth and death (OK... Three things... Taxes)... These things we have no control over -- especially taxes! Seriously... We have absolutely nothing to say about our birth and very little to say about our death... Sure, we can eat healthy, exercise, stay away from all the things that are bad for us like. But sooner or later, no matter what we do, we're going to die.

The trick is to understand that between birth and death, we have control over most of the decisions we have to make.

Our God gives us the freedom to make our decisions... Good or bad. We can ask for help, sure, but ultimately, we end up making the decision. We can decide whether or not to be Christians, how to live our life, what jobs we choose... We're not puppets of a God who controls every move we make.

Who's in control here?

You can't control the length of your life, but you can control its use.
You can't control the way your face is shaped, but you can control its expressions.
You can't control people's annoying habits, but you can make sure you don't get similar ones.

Are you letting life and all the things that happen in it control you? Or are you controlling your life and how you react to situations with God's help? I hope it's the second one... I hope that you realize that to make good decisions, with important things like whether or not to be a Christian, or simple things like whether to smile and say hello to a stranger, you need God's guidance.

Don't worry about the things you can't control... Get busy controlling the things that depend on you. Be honest with yourself and God. Have you been striving to be the person God wants you to be? Who is in control of YOUR life?

Day 163

 What then? Shall we sin because we are not under law but under grace? By no means! Don't you know that when you offer yourselves to someone to obey him as slaves, you are slaves to the one whom you obey -- whether you are slaves to sin, which leads to death, or to obedience, which leads to righteousness? Romans 6:15-16

Don't Compromise!

The word compromise has a few different meanings... The settlement of differences by mutual concessions; a middle course -- something intermediate; expose to suspicion or scandal (make a compromise).

For today, we'll be thinking about the last definition... The pressure to compromise our beliefs is one of the biggest challenges ever... And we all face it... We all deal with situations where we have to decide right from wrong...

A young person might have to deal with the pressure to have a beer at a party or smoke or whether to cheat on a test... An older person may have to decide whether or not to take a short cut in a business deal to make extra money knowing it's wrong...

What to do...

We're all faced with situations that may force us to compromise our faith. I think we get put in these situations for a variety of reasons... Peer pressure, self-pressure, greed, no money...

But as Christians, we have to struggle not to give in to those pressures... Believe me, I know how hard it is to stand out from the crowd... And sometimes it's just easier to give in to the pressures and do the wrong things.

So, since all of us struggle with this issue of compromise, I came up with a few thoughts to help you get through the day...

- Choose friends carefully. Everyone you spend time with has an influence on you...
- Remember that you are unique
- Pleasing God is better than pleasing your friends

Day 164

> I have been crucified with Christ and I no longer live, but Christ lives in me. The life I live in the body, I live by faith in the Son of God, who loved me and gave himself for me.
> Galatians 2:20

Breaking News

Headline: People judge Christianity and Christians by looking at you.

Read that again... It's important. People everywhere form opinions about Christians and Christianity by watching your actions and seeing how you live your life.

Think about it for a second... If you see someone smoking you might make an instant judgment about that person. If you see someone wearing old clothes and sitting on a park bench in the middle of the day you might form an opinion about that person. If you see someone stealing something... OK... You get the idea...

If you form opinions...

Since I have the talent of pointing out the obvious, I'll go ahead and do it again. If you look at other people and come to conclusions about them, do you think people do the same thing when they watch someone who claims to be a Christian?

If you're talking to someone and you swear, drink alcohol, and do drugs, then while the cigarette in your hand is still burning, tell that person how you got away with cheating on a test, stole money from your parents... What will that person think when you tell him you're a Christian? Do you think he'll have a good feeling about Christians?

Other people do the same when seeing how you live your life. Once you're a Christian, you change. Outwardly you stay the same... It's not like you have a mark on your forehead or anything... Your personality may not change... But on the inside you're a new person. You're a representative of Jesus everywhere you go.

People are watching you... Do you think Christ lives in you? If someone looks at you what do you think they see? You're a walking, talking advertisement for Jesus... Keep that in mind everywhere you go.

Day 165

> Let them give thanks to the Lord for his unfailing love and his wonderful deeds for men. Psalm 107:21

Turkey 'N Football

OK... Maybe turkey and football isn't exactly the same, but when my 'not-so-mighty' Detroit Lions play on Thanksgiving, I've been known to call them turkey's... Along with other things...

On Thanksgiving, it's easy to get caught up in family gatherings, eating lots of food, watching football, playing games, and watching parades... Why do we do all these things only on Thanksgiving Day? Maybe because if we ate everyday like we do on Thanksgiving, we wouldn't be able to fit through the doors!

But seriously... We do all these things on Thanksgiving... Is this what Thanksgiving is really about?? OK... I'll be honest with you... I'd be thankful if the Lions could win once in a while on Thanksgiving...

Be thankful!

So if Thanksgiving is about more than family gatherings, turkey, ham, veggies, rolls, cranberry sauce, and football... What exactly is Thanksgiving? Isn't every day Thanksgiving Day?

Thanksgiving is gratitude towards God. Thanksgiving should be expressed everyday in the lives of a Christian. God has blessed us with so much... Homes, food, clothing, cars, loving families... (Is it too much to ask for a winning season for the Lions??) With all these luxuries, how often do you take time out to thank God? If you're like most people, you probably don't do that enough.

Lets stop complaining... Lets thank God for his blessings every day, not just one day in November. Let's take time out to really thank God for all the wonderful things in our lives. Go beyond the same old things you say at the table every year... Thank God for everything big and small...

Day 166

> He will wipe every tear from their eyes. There will be no more death or mourning or crying or pain, for the old order of things has passed away. He who was seated on the throne said, "I am making everything new!" Then he said, "Write this down, for these words are trustworthy and true."
>
> Revelation 21:4-5

The Lions Win!!

You may know what a HUGE fan I am of the Detroit Lion's football team... Every year they're horrible. They haven't won many games... Every year on Thanksgiving Day, they play... It's a tradition... It's also a tradition to lose on Thanksgiving...

On Thanksgiving Day, 2003, the Lions beat the Green Bay Packers... It was a great football game. The Lions played the game with a lot of energy and emotion and they beat a fantastic team.

Every year the Lions manage to win one game... And every year, I hear: "This is the turning point for us... We're not looking back at last week or last year... We're looking forward..."

Look forward!

When people drive, they have to focus on the road in front of them, not look in the rear view mirror; runners have to focus on the finish line, not on where they've been; football teams that have losing seasons year after year have to look forward, not at last weeks or last season's failure.

As Christians, we need to focus on our relationships with God; on our mission to spread the word of Jesus... We need to focus on living good lives and doing the right thing... Not on the mistakes that we made yesterday... Nothing good can come from dwelling on the past... Focus your energy on doing the right thing TODAY and TOMORROW. We can all learn a lesson from the Detroit Lions... Obviously we shouldn't learn football from them, but we can learn to focus on the present and the future...

All the things we've done wrong, all the sin, (missed tackles, dropped passes) are in the past. It's a new season!

Day 167

> For though a righteous man falls seven times, he rises again, but the wicked are brought down by calamity. Proverbs 24:16

Ouch!

I'll just let you in on a secret... Not that you don't already know this... Falling down hurts... Now you can't say I never told you anything...

Falling down can mean a lot of things... Actually falling, maybe off a bike or skateboard... Maybe falling down and not doing well with studies; having an idea that didn't work out... The point is falling down can mean a lot of things to a lot of people...

I've fallen a lot... When I was a kid I got hit playing baseball, as a young adult I got rejected asking girls for dates, as an adult I've fallen more times than I care to admit.

Failure is a growing experience

If I hadn't fallen in all the areas of life that I have... I wouldn't be where I am today... If I hadn't been forced to get back in the game and swing at a baseball after getting hit I wouldn't have all the great baseball memories...

Falling, although it stinks, is part of life. If you don't fall you can't grow as a person... Falling doesn't equal failure... It's just one of those things that goes along with life.

As a Christian you will sometimes fall flat on your face. If you don't get up and continue on the Christian walk then you can't expect to grow in your faith. But if you get up, determined to continue on, you will. You aren't perfect and you don't live in a perfect world... Even the people you consider to be strong Christians are going to fall, or have fallen already! You WILL fall at some point... But it's your decision to get up and dust yourself off or stay down...

What will you do?

Day 168

> To Adam he said, "Because you listened to your wife and ate from the tree about which I commanded you, 'You must not eat of it,' Cursed is the ground because of you; through painful toil you will eat of it all the days of your life."
> Genesis 3:17

'Cuz I Said So...

Sometimes obeying people in authority, whether it be parents, teachers or anyone else, seems like a real hassle. Why do you think those people set rules for us and tell us what to do and what not to do?

I can remember purposely disobeying my parents as a teen. I'm sure my mom can come up with a list a mile long of all the times I did things directly after one of my parents told me not to do it... But...

I'll just tell you about one of the things I remember... It was a beautiful Spring week in Michigan... I mentioned that I'd really like to go to school in the morning and skip the afternoon so I could go play golf... My dad made it very clear that he thought it was a bad idea... I thought I could get away with it...

The consequences...

To make a long story short, I got caught... I forget what the punishment was, but there was some penalty for my offense. In our Bible verse today, Adam got caught and his penalty was pretty severe... In verse 17 God tells Adam his punishment was that he'd have to work hard on the land to get his food.

Think for a minute about when you disobeyed a parent. Why do you think you do it? What are the penalties for disobeying? If you don't get caught, was disobeying OK? Why do you think your parents (or teachers) make rules? What gives them the power to enforce them?

Today, (and every day!) I want to challenge you to make an effort to listen to the authority figures in your life. Make an honest effort. Think about what you can do to show them that you're really making a change in your life and that you're going to start showing them respect and listen to their rules... Tell them today that you understand why they make rules for you... Because they love you.

Day 169

 When they kept on questioning him, he straightened up and said to them, "If any one of you is without sin, let him be the first to throw a stone at her." John 8:7

If You Live In A Glass House...

"People who live in glass houses should not throw stones", "That's like the pot calling the kettle black", "It takes one to know one". Maybe you've heard these sayings before. They're really just a different way of saying that sometimes people criticize other people when they may be guilty of the same kinds of things.

One of my friends is a pretty mellow kind of guy... Very laid-back. He doesn't really worry about much, and gets things done at his own pace and on his own schedule. His wife constantly gets after him about getting projects done (or even started) because he's a procrastinator...

I like to make comments about projects that he started and never got around to finishing... "Hey... How's the bathroom remodeling coming along?" knowing that he hasn't done anything since the last time I asked... His wife always says that he and I get along so well because I'm the same way... So it 'takes one to know one'.

Don't throw stones

The verse from John was taken from part of a story where a woman was in trouble for committing adultery. She was brought before a bunch of men who wanted to stone her, which was the common punishment. That's where Jesus said, "If any one of you is without sin, let him be the first to throw a stone at her."

Sometimes it's so easy to "throw stones" at people for mistakes they make. It's easy for us to judge someone for sinning, whether it be telling lies, or stealing or anything else. But lets not forget... We all make mistakes... We all live in "glass houses"... If we throw stones at them, who's to stop someone from throwing stones at us? We're no better then those people.

Have you thrown stones at anyone lately? I think we need to help people see the sins they've committed, but out of love, not in a hurtful way... And I think we should expect our friends to do the same to us, even though it's hard to hear sometimes.

Day 170

 For God so loved the world that he gave his one and only Son, that whoever believes in him shall not perish but have eternal life. John 3:16

Make A List

The holidays are coming... Can you believe it? Whether it's February, July or November, It seems like Christmas is right around the corner and before you know it, we'll all be thinking about what we want... We'll be in "holiday spending" mode!

People will be scurrying around the malls and stores looking for the perfect gifts... Well, not me... It isn't December 24 yet... But maybe you will... You'll have a wish list, probably get one from your parents or brothers and sisters and you'll have to decide what to buy off the list.

Toys R Us and all the other stores will put out their Holiday Wish list catalogs so you can find something for everyone on your list. Some catalogs are filled with gifts for "People who have everything"... Every year I go through the lists, trying to figure out who I've bought for and who I've forgotten...

Missing list

Of course we've all heard the Christmas story over and over again... This year, with all the "stuff" that's being bought for the special people in our lives, we might forget the one REALLY special person... You know... The one who started it all...

But what do you give a God who has everything? Somehow in all the "wish lists" I always manage to be missing one... I have a list from all the members of my family, from Maggie the dog, from friends at school and work... But I often forget about God's "Wish List".

God has everything... Every toy, CD, book, stereo, video game... But even with instant access to all the material things that are on our wish lists, He only caress about one thing... You. He wants what no amount of money can buy and which only you can give: your life and your heart. Think about what you'll be getting God, but don't wait for December 25 to give it.

Day 171

 Some time later God tested Abraham. He said to him, "Abraham!" "Here I am," he replied. Then God said, "Take your son, your only son, Isaac, whom you love, and go to the region of Moriah. Sacrifice him there as a burnt offering on one of the mountains I will tell you about." Genesis 22:1-2

You Call That A Test?

You probably know I'm a college student... No wise cracks about being the oldest college student, please... I take tests and final exams just like everyone else... I'm not the sharpest knife in the drawer, but I study hard and prepare as best as I can for these huge tests...

Some of the classes I've done better in than others, so it's no surprise to me that studying for some of the finals has been easier than others. But, when it's time to take a test, all the hard work pays off...

I don't know about you, but when I have to take a big test, I get all nervous, have a hard time sleeping the night before, get up REALLY early, pace around, look at the clock... And that's before I ever get to class! Once I'm there? Anxious, sweating, tapping my foot and fingers... The pressure is unbelievable... Will I choose the right answers?

A real test

As stressful as all this is, it isn't anything like the test God had for Abraham. HELLOOOO... Sacrifice your son? No questions asked? Are you kidding me?

Later in the chapter, Abraham chooses to listen to God... He takes his son, ties him up and places him on an altar... But is stopped by an angel of the Lord... But he was willing to listen. He passed the test.

There are times in our lives when we are given tests. Some of them are small tests to see if we'll listen to God... Others are more difficult to follow. Sometimes it seems like it's easier to ignore the tests and go our own way... Think about what would happen if we all sought the glory of God like Abraham did... Sure, there will be times when your faith is tested... Choose to glorify God and you'll pass the test every single time.

Day 172

> The Lord detests the thoughts of the wicked, but those of the pure are pleasing to him. Proverbs 15:26

Alone With Your Thoughts

When you're all alone... You know... Nobody bothering you, no pets in your way, no noise, no homework or other distractions... What do you think about?

School, parents, relationships, work, sports, friends, music, TV, clothes, money, cars, movies, your next date, your last date, the weekend, Monday morning, what's for dinner, what you want, talking on the phone, going to a concert, driving, community service hours, graduating...

Today's verse talks about wicked and pure thoughts. Can you think of some examples of wicked and pure thoughts? Don't feel bad... Everyone has both of these kinds of thoughts... On the wicked side maybe you'll have lies, swearing, or pornography. On the pure side, maybe you have loving your parents or anticipating singing in church.

If you have a thought, but nobody knows about it, did you really think something?

I think the fact that our thoughts are secret, known only to us, gives us an excuse out to think whatever we want... For example... Maybe I'm walking in the mall and I see a great video game that I'd like to have but don't have the money for... Maybe the thought crosses my mind that I could steal the game and have lots of fun playing it at home...

Pure thought? No. Would I act on it? No. Was it the right thing to think? No. But since I didn't tell anyone, I don't have that guilty feeling that I would have if I told someone and they said, "Joel... That isn't a very good thing to think."

Don't get caught in this trap. Don't think that because it's just a random thought, and nobody knows about it that it's OK to have those bad thoughts. Just remember that God knows your every thought, so those thoughts aren't exactly a secret.

Day 173

 But we have this treasure in jars of clay to show that this all-surpassing power is from God and not from us. We are hard pressed on every side, but not crushed; perplexed, but not in despair; persecuted, but not abandoned; struck down, but not destroyed. 2 Corinthians 4:7-9

Those Ugly Clay Pots

A hundred years ago, when I was in grade school, we made art projects out of clay... Being as un-artistic as I am, my projects always turned out really ugly. Most of the time, I'm certain nobody really knew what they were.

I remember a specific project I did for my dad for Fathers Day. It was this terribly ugly "candy dish"... OK.. It was really just an open thing with the sides turned up kind of like a bowl... But I called it a candy dish and gave it to him proudly.

Maybe it was his job, as my dad, or maybe just the nice thing to do... But he put my candy dish right on his desk, filled it with candy, and kept it there for years... Long after I was out of school, in fact. When people were in his office, they looked past the fact that the candy dish was plain and ugly and took candy from it anyway.

There's a treasure in those ugly pots!

Sometimes I think the best place to hide things is right in the open. I know people who have been robbed... Had everything in their jewelry boxes thrown around while the really valuable necklaces were right on the dining room table in plain site! I also know people who hid diamonds in the freezer with the ice cubes!

People who lived during the time the Bible was written didn't have freezers to hide their valuables in, but even back then, thieves wouldn't look in the most obvious places. People put valuables in ordinary looking clay pots and the thieves often ignored those things thinking they weren't valuable.

Maybe we should look at ourselves as ordinary clay pots... God put treasure inside us... He gave us talents and gifts that can be used to glorify His kingdom. Sometimes Satan comes along hoping to steal our treasure and use it for his gain, but we have to rely on God to keep those treasures safe... Which he does! I want to challenge you to use your talents and gifts to glorify God today and every day.

Day 174

> But the Lord said to Samuel, "Do not consider his appearance or his height, for I have rejected him. The Lord does not look at the things man looks at. Man looks at the outward appearance, but the Lord looks at the heart." 1 Samuel 16:7

Inner vs. Outer

How much time do you spend standing in front of the mirror in the morning? I bet when you go through your morning routine part of that is checking everything out in the mirror. I don't spend 10 seconds fixing my hair, but that's a different story...

Most people spend time fixing everything because every place we look we see beautiful people... Magazines, television, movies, music videos... Everywhere! All these images encourage us to spend a lot of time looking in the mirror, be on diets, exercise and be gorgeous.

I think it was a line from a movie from a long time ago, "Beauty may only be skin deep, but ugly goes all the way to the bone!" How terrible is that comment?

Outer beauty is only skin deep

When I was in high school, I had a friend named Kory. He had absolutely everything going for him. He was an incredible athlete, brilliant student, good looking, popular guy with tons of friends... Everyone wanted to be around him.

Kory had a terrible accident. He was cleaning something with gasoline and somehow started a fire. A huge percentage of his body was burned. He was in the hospital for months recovering... His outer beauty was long gone... And so were all the people who wanted to be around him. His personality hadn't changed... He was still a great guy, but people couldn't get beyond the burns and scars.

The phrase 'You can't judge a book by its cover' comes to mind. If you saw Kory walking down the street today, you might ignore him or walk away or turn your head... And you'd be missing out on knowing an amazing person. Outward beauty is temporary and fades away... But what is on the inside is forever... That's what really counts. When you look at people, look beyond outer beauty and get to know that person for what's really important... Their inner beauty.

Day 175

{ For wisdom will enter your heart, and knowledge will be pleasant to your soul. Proverbs 2:10 }

Back When I Was Your Age...

I had to WALK to school... With bare feet, in ten feet of snow, uphill both ways! I worked all week for 5 cents! I didn't have TV... We had to make our own fun! I didn't have a baseball bat, we used broom handles!

You've probably heard some of these things before... Maybe from your parents or grandparents, maybe from teachers. But how often do we really listen to the adults in our lives?

My dad was a brilliant man. He didn't go to college, but he was one of the smartest people I had the pleasure of knowing. What made him brilliant wasn't just that he knew a lot of facts and bits of information, but he had experienced so many things!

Learn something new today

He always had lots of stories about things he had done or seen. Most of the time I thought I knew better and didn't really listen. As I got older, I started to realize that he was really teaching me things that I would never learn in history books.

Fortunately I came to that realization a few years before he passed away, so I had the opportunity to really listen to him... But I missed learning so many things because I didn't take the time to listen to someone with wisdom that can only come from years of living.

I want to urge you to take advantage of the life lessons that you can learn from... Your grandparents... Older people in your church and community, even your parents and teachers... Can teach you things, through their stories, that you will never, ever learn in school. Take time to talk to them... You'll learn something, brighten their day, and be able to pass along the knowledge of past generations to the future generations.

Day 176

> All scripture is God-breathed and is useful for teaching, rebuking, correcting and training in righteousness.
> 2 Timothy 3:16

World Wide Best Seller

Sometimes I get calls from relatives asking me about what I'd like as a gift... "We did most of our shopping for you, but we need to get one more little thing... Do you have any suggestions?"

Suggestions? Me? Oh man, do I have suggestions... New cymbals, a DVD player, new printer (OK... a whole new computer!), PS2 games... Oh... Wait... "A little thing"...

There is one thing that I'd really like to have... It's been a "Best Seller" for years... A story with love, hate, miracles, tragedy joy and suspense... All things necessary to make an interesting story. If I was thinking about movies that I want, I don't think I could find one that combined all these plots, stories and characters. I don't think there's a movie that could hold my interest as well as this particular "little thing" - but nobody every thinks to put it on their list of stuff they want.

Take time to read... The Bible!

There are things in life that I haven't figured out yet... What would dogs say if they could talk? Why do songs all sound the same? Who decided that 10 items in the express lane was the right number? Girls <-- that I'll REALLY never figure out.

But you know what? There's a place where I can turn to learn about the important things in life... Kinda like "Life's Instruction Manual" -- the Bible. It's a great book! If I need guidance, support, comfort or to feel loved... There's a verse that will help me!

Get in the habit of reading the Bible every day. Take 5 minutes out of your day to read the Bible... And if you don't have one that is easy to understand, ask someone to give you a new Bible as a gift... Let every step in your life be tested by the Bible.

Day 177

 If you confess with your mouth, "Jesus is Lord," and believe in your heart that God raised him from the dead, you will be saved. Romans 10:9

Are You Or Aren't You?

I've gone through most of my life 'knowing' I was a Christian. I grew up in a Christian home, went to church, went to a Christian school, prayed at dinner and before bed... I was a Christian.

Or was I? I went through the motions, tried to do the right thing, sang in the youth choir (Yeah, yeah... I used to sing... Now I make noises like a sick cow). I was told I was a Christian when I was a young kid, baptized as a baby... I was a Christian.

The truth is, I couldn't remember ever truly accepting Jesus as my Savior and saying, "I love you, God! And I want to spend my life living for you!" ... That was a tough realization for me because I "had been a Christian" all my life. But at that moment, I re-dedicated my life and started paying attention to the plan God has for me.

So... Are you or aren't you a Christian?

This is a message for you and everyone you know... No matter where you are on your "Walk With God", I'm telling you today that you need to think about your life and how you're living it. Maybe you're a "better Christian" than I was, maybe you're just starting in your faith, maybe you're somewhere right in between...

I mess up. Do you? But we can have eternal life... We have to admit we mess up... Don't feel bad, you're not alone! All you have to do is ask for forgiveness, understand that Jesus died and rose again, be willing to give your life to Jesus, and invite Him into your heart.

If you're ready, pray right now... Heavenly Father, I come to you hoping to leave my sinful life behind and to come to You for salvation and the promise of eternal life. Lord, I know that I mess up but I'm asking you for forgiveness. I believe that Your Son died for me, and I want to spend the rest of my life serving you. In Jesus name I pray. AMEN.

Day 178

> "Now go; I will help you speak and will teach you what to say." Exodus 4:12

Bring A Friend

I've been challenging you to think about your life and re-commit to God... I've also been challenging you to give your friends an opportunity to change their lives. I hope that you've been able to find comfort in these messages of salvation.

I bet if I called all the people who are reading this book and asked if they talk to friends and relatives about God, some would say yes... And a lot of people would say no. I've been wondering why, if all of us know people who are non-Christians, and all of us love Jesus, why doesn't EVERYONE talk to at least one person?

Maybe it's because we don't want our friends and relatives to think we're "Church Geeks", maybe it's because we don't want people to know we're Christians because they'll think we don't know how to have fun, maybe it's because...

We don't know what to say...

I'm guilty... I write these thoughts, and don't feel bad about sharing God with you... Because you or someone you know bought the book... But at my home church, we have "Bring a Friend To Church" day... Now, I know a LOT of people, but instead of asking people who don't go to church, I ask friends who I know will come as a favor to me... Why?

Maybe I want to be cool, popular, don't want people to laugh at me... But the truth is, maybe I'm just afraid that those people HAVE noticed that I'm different, and want to know what I've got... Then what do I tell them?

In Exodus, we're told that God will give us the words we need to tell people about our faith... Earlier in Exodus, Moses is spoken to by a burning bush... Now, I'm not telling you that you're going to get the words like that... But be sure, if the opportunity comes up to tell someone about God, you'll do just fine... So bring a friend to faith today.

Day 179

 Be self-controlled and alert. Your enemy the devil prowls around like a roaring lion looking for someone to devour. Resist him, standing firm in the faith, because you know that your brothers throughout the world are undergoing the same kind of sufferings. 1 Peter 5:8-9

A Crack In The Wall

Not that long ago, a contractor came into my apartment to fix the wall in the bathroom. The wall was falling down... Literally! The paint had peeled off and the drywall underneath had gotten all soft and started falling down. All because of the steam from the shower.

He patched it back up and made it look just like new. He even went around the rest of the bathroom and fixed all the other spots that looked weak. He told me the walls had to dry before he could paint. When I looked in there, after he had left, the walls and ceilings looked smooth and solid.

The next day he was back. Within thirty minutes the room smelled like fresh paint and looked brand new. He had transformed the bathroom from a run down room into a brand new clean one. You couldn't even see where he made the repairs.

A cat on the prowl

The next morning when I took my shower, I looked up and saw a spot. Right where he had patched. In less than a week, the wall came crashing down again. Even though the repair guy fixed the wall, there was a weakness where he had to patch.

Our lives are sometimes like my wall. We sin, ask God to forgive us, and are restored to brand new. But Satan knows where our weaknesses are and that's right where he goes! He wiggles in those cracks and we end up falling into the same sins all over again.

Today, I want to leave you with a different kind of thought. An uplifting one. One of my favorite benedictions; I hope you find it as inspiring as I do... "And the God of all grace, who called you to his eternal glory in Christ, after you have suffered for a little while, will himself restore you and make you strong, firm and steadfast. To him be the power for ever and ever. Amen." (1 Peter 5:10)

Day 180

> But when envoys were sent by the rulers of Babylon to ask him about the miraculous sign that had occurred in the land, God left him to test him and to know everything that was in his heart. 2 Chronicles 32:31

Pass / Fail

Have you ever stopped to think about how you react to things? Situations? Problems? People? Have you ever thought about the decisions you have to make every day? Not why you make a decision... But why you have decisions to make?

Think about some of the decisions you have to make in a regular day. Mom comes to wake you up. Do you yell at her or get up in a good mood. You walk outside and it's raining. Do you think, "Alright! Another day from God." Or, "Awww, man! Rain again, God?"

What do you hate the most about school? For me, there is nothing worse than taking tests. Just the thought of tests makes my heart race. I know the material but when I take the test, somehow all the information flies out of my brain and I don't know which answer to choose. Why do all teachers give tests?

Life is a test

Could it be that all these decisions we make are part of some big test from God? Do you think God is watching our decisions? Attitudes? Is God testing us like the teachers at school? Ack! Everyday my life is part of a multiple-choice test.

Look at all the people in the Bible who were tested by God. Starting with Adam and Eve! How about David? Adam and Eve didn't pass, David didn't always pass. Today's verse is referring to Hezekiah. When he was questioned, God left because he wanted to see how Hezekiah would react. It was a test.

Life is a test. Every situation we're put in, like the ones above, or how we react to unanswered prayers or sickness, is part of a test. The good news is God isn't sitting with the "red pen" ready to fail us. He wants us all to pass the tests. He never gives us any test we can't pass. He's ready to give you an "A" and reward you for it in Heaven. You can prove you're ready for God's plan by passing his tests.

Personal Journal: Thoughts, ideas, questions

Personal Journal: Thoughts, ideas, questions

Printed in the United States
30536LVS00002B/23